The
Wounded
Minister

Books by Guy Greenfield

The Wounded Minister

Healing from and Preventing Personal Attacks

Guy Greenfield, Ph.D.

Foreword by Dr. Brooks Faulkner

Baker Books

A Division of Baker Book House Co
Grand Rapids, Michigan 49516

Published by Baker Books
a division of Baker Book House Company
P.O. Box 6287, Grand Rapids, MI 49516-6287

Printed in the United States of America

Library of Congress Cataloging-in-Publication Data

Greenfield, Guy.
    The wounded minister : healing from and preventing personal
attacks / Guy Greenfield ; foreword by Brooks Faulkner.
      p.   cm.
    Includes bibliographical references.
    ISBN 0-8010-6369-8 (pbk.)
    1. Clergy—Abuse of. 2. Clergy—Psychology. 3. Church
controversies. I. Title.
    BV4398.G74   2001
    253'.2—dc21
                                    2001025945

For current information about all releases from Baker Book House, visit our
web site:
                    http://www.bakerbooks.com

To Shirley

Who taught me the healing power of laughter and joy

Contents

Foreword

This is not a book for the weak-hearted. It is a no-nonsense look at the hurts, pains, unadulterated anger, and ultimate redemption of a struggling minister who battled the demons within the church and within himself and won. It is a modern-day Howard Cosell who "tells it like it is" without shading it with diplomatic clichés and warm fuzzies. It is a Bunyanesque journey of a Christian's pilgrimage through the gates of a metaphorical Hades as a pastor and minister into the realm of forgiveness and understanding.

I found myself fighting the same villains as the author. I was angry along with him. I was insulted along with him. I was hurt along with him. I was humiliated along with him. I was lonely along with him. I was in despair along with him. The author has the gift of helping the reader crawl into the casket and feel the Lazarus pull that cancels the funeral and starts the wedding.

The Wounded Minister is cathartic. It takes the minister into surgery. It reveals the cancer. It displays the malignancy. But then it does what any good reading does. It helps the surgery succeed into potential spiritual health. The humanity of the author is not disguised. He sheds the sanctimonious shield of superficial spirituality and lets the reader see the raw ugliness that results when good people are hurt by bad intentions from unscrupulous church members. If you can read this book without feeling the catharsis of new passion and regeneration of personhood, you have long lost the sheer exuberance of eating ice cream.

This is also a story of Everyman in ministry. It is the minister who is terminated and struggles to find reasons why. It is the minister who is succeeding in every aspect of ministry but at the cost of self-respect, for not standing for the right things at the right time. It is the minister who is morally bankrupt but searching for new directions after admitting, "All have sinned, but I never thought it would be me." It is a story of Everyman and a road to travel at the speed of Heinz, not the autobahn.

But it is a story of hope. At age sixty-two, when the walls crumbled and the author was all but terminated, he asked, *What can a man expect at this age and at such a time as this?* Financially pressed and with a bleak future, he fought back and now in his late sixties gives even more meaning to his life in the November and December years of his ministry. He takes us through the haze of forgiveness into the bright lights of purpose, meaning, and direction.

The author does not leave the reader hanging. He ties the knot so that the package will hold. His ultimate purpose is described pointedly in the introduction, where he says that the major purpose is for "wounded ministers to recover from their shattered vocational dreams and to find their way back into an active and supportive ministry in the church or in one of its agencies." You should not put this book down until you have read chapters 11 through 14. The heart of recovery is there. Describing the malignancy is more than adequately done in the first ten chapters, but the genius of the book is in chapters 11 through 14.

Dr. Greenfield gives four strong remedies but the prescription prices are expensive: Restrengthen your faith, listen again to your call, be creative, and replace dysfunctional core beliefs. The prognosis is possible but the probability of passionate implementation may be questionable. The jury is still out, and only the strong willed among recovering ministers will adopt a new pattern of spiritual and psychological health.

Chapter 14 describes ways the wounded healer can become an encourager for one's fellow abused minister. Truly, ministers need each other.

Chapter 9 defines traits that tend to get the wounded minister in hot water. Neurosis is defined in terms of how the minister relates to others and also perceives himself. How can a minister deal with his own anger? What about narcissism? Is it reality or perception in the minds of those who are looking for ammunition to bring the minister down? And, also, can a church deal redemptively with the overly emotional (unstable) and attention-seeking minister? A salty look at the bully tendencies of some as well as the ADD (attention deficit disorder) minister makes captivating reading.

All those staff members who are not senior pastors will want to pay close attention to chapter 10, for it is in this chapter where the author answers the question for the reader, "Who will battle for the common man (staff member) when abuse is apparent?"

Then, almost as an afterthought but certainly a poignant afterthought, the author concludes in the afterword that the only reconstructive and redemptive process is to "stop whining" and get on with the call.

This is exciting reading. This is gripping drama. But it truly is the yellow brick road that leads back to Kansas. For the minister who is lost in the maze of self-destruction after a tornadic termination, this book is for you. For the counselor who is looking for pragmatic answers to inflammatory questions in a minister-client's life, this book is for you. For the wounded minister's spouse who is trying to understand what is going on, this book is for you too. And, just as important, for those church members who are trying to be conciliatory with their new pastor after taking termination detours with other pastors in their church, this book is for you.

Dr. Brooks Faulkner
Senior Specialist, LeaderCare
LifeWay Christian Resources
Nashville, Tennessee

Introduction

Emotionally, this is a very difficult book for me to write. I am a "wounded minister" from the front ranks of the battle of church conflict. Although it has been a few years since I was wounded in the ministry, if I allow myself to think about it, I can still feel some anger over what I experienced. It should never have happened. I did not ask for it. I did not anticipate it. It just happened—gradually over a period of three years.

Today I can say that I have dealt with much of the bitterness I once felt and have risen above it by the grace of God. This book is an attempt to show others how to do this for themselves. However, I want to say up front, before exposing some of the harsh realities wounded ministers have faced, that most churches are full of wonderful and loving laypersons who care deeply for their ministers. The problems on which I am focusing are caused by a very small percentage of persons, yet these few cause horrendous damage in the life of the church. This book is an attempt to do something constructive about the abused and the abusers.

My Experience of Abuse

Looking back, I must admit that I was somewhat naive about how conflict and division take place in a church. I found myself at age fifty-nine being called to a church that had a history of conflict. Over a period of twenty-five years, this church had had seven ministers, not one of whom had had a pleasant exit. On my arrival there, I had no idea that I would become number eight. The pastor search committee had simply told me that they needed "an older man with a lot of experience." I felt I qualified and they

13

agreed. Ninety-six percent of the congregation voted to invite me to be their minister. I later learned that was the highest percentage of a vote they had ever given a minister.

Within my first year, I began to realize that I had made a very serious mistake. No one told me this; I simply began to read the signs of a long-standing conflicted atmosphere. One former member, an attorney, told me he believed the church "was possessed by an evil spirit who influenced different people at different times over the years of the church's history." At first, I thought this was a somewhat harsh evaluation. Three years later, I had concluded that he was probably closer to the truth than I had wanted to believe.

Within two years I became the victim of what some call a "clergy killer" and others call a "pathological antagonist." This man was able to pull together a small group of sympathizers who together created such turmoil in the congregation that by age sixty-two I decided to take early retirement and get out of a very unhealthy situation. My health indeed began to deteriorate to the point that my personal physician advised me to resign and do something else. I had already had a triple bypass heart operation some ten years earlier. Stress could bring on another one or worse. I could have stayed; I had the votes to keep me in my position as the pastor, but it would not have been worth it. I was not Jesus. This church was not worth my dying for.

During my first year as pastor, this clergy killer began to orchestrate his way into several key positions of leadership in the church. As a member of the nominating committee, he was able to place himself in these various positions. He soon held more leadership positions than any other member of the church. With his power base in place, he launched his attacks on me.

All during this time, I began to alert several other leaders of the church about what was happening. To a person, they told me there was nothing to worry about. They could handle any problems that might arise. When the problems began to arise, these good but naive people said that prayer could solve these difficulties. "The Lord will take care of it." In fact they did next to nothing but allowed the antagonist freedom and room to operate. So he took full advantage of their passivity. The attacks increased. A full campaign of letter-writing and phone calls began to wreck the unity and peace of the fellowship.

Meeting with this man privately proved to be futile. He made promises of support that he didn't intend to keep. Then I took other respected leaders with me but to no avail. I met with small clusters of supportive people. I could tell they did not have the stomach for confrontation and conflict. I felt very much alone.

This was a heavy blow to my ego. For over a decade I had been a full professor with tenure at the largest theological graduate school in the world. I had earlier served successful pastorates with pleasant exits each time I left. I had never experienced forced termination. I had been loved, respected, and admired by most of the people in those pastorates. I was the author of five successful books. One of these titles had been a national best-seller and translated into two foreign languages. I had never had any major problems in any of my former ministry positions. But my last pastorate was a different story. There I faced for the first time a clergy killer and some pathological antagonists. I became severely wounded in a battle I had not anticipated.

Since leaving that pastorate, I have discovered that throughout the ranks of the ministry I am not alone. There are numerous wounded ministers, and this large number of abused clergy cuts across most all denominational lines. It is a plague that afflicts the church at large.

This problem is a growing phenomenon. Numerous publications of observations and research indicate that it is in fact a major problem approaching crisis proportions. Talk to any group of ministers, and you will hear stories of tragedy and heartache. In recent years I have interviewed a considerable number of former ministers, now in secular work, and nearly everyone I talked with told me a similar story that resulted in forced termination. Many of them are now cynical, bitter, angry, and discouraged. Most tell me they will never return to a full-time paid church position. Their wounds continue to be painful.

The winter 1996 issue of *Leadership* reports a national survey of Protestant clergy that revealed 23 percent of ministers report they have been fired at least once, and 43 percent said that a "faction" (usually fewer than ten persons) forced them to resign. Only a few antagonists are needed to cause substantial havoc and devastation. This same report also indicated that 41 percent of congregations who fired their pastor had done so at least twice before. The stated reasons for forced termination vary considerably: personality conflicts (43 percent), conflicting visions for the church (17 percent), financial strain in the congregation (7 percent), theological differences (5 percent), moral dereliction (5 percent), unrealistic expectations (4 percent), and miscellaneous reasons (19 percent).

In my own denomination (Southern Baptist), it has regularly been reported that between 2,000 and 2,500 ministers are forced out of the ministry each year. Other denominations as well as independent churches are reporting similar problems of significant magnitude.

The Nature of Abuse

This book is an attempt to explain the disturbing nature of ministerial abuse and what can be done about it. By using the term *minister* I am including ordained persons in any type of church vocational ministry: pastors, associate pastors, ministers of education, ministers of music, church administrators, ministers to youth and/or students, and ministers to various age groups and family structures, including singles.

I will describe the culprits who lead in the abuse of ministers: "clergy killers," "pathological antagonists," "well-intentioned dragons," and other troublesome persons who are emotionally and/or mentally disturbed.

Some will be critical of my use of these labels of antagonistic dysfunctionality. Some recent authors have disdained the labeling of anyone in the church as a "killer," an "antagonist," or a "dragon." They argue that labels block reconciliation and cooperation and prevent the resolution of church conflicts. Consequently I need to say here in the beginning that I am not writing about normal church conflict. Several specialists in church-conflict resolution have written tremendously helpful works to guide churches through these divisive situations.

Specifically, I am writing about evil, mean-spirited persons who are able to inflict disastrous wounds on unsuspecting ministers in the name of religion and "for God." I am a recent trooper from the battlefield of bloody confrontation who tried to be pastoral, loving, understanding, reconciling, and redemptive yet ended up being shot down and left to die on the battlefield of the church, and there are thousands just like me.

Labeling is a necessary part of communication and understanding. It is an important function of language. All disciplines practice labeling—the sciences, history, philosophy, psychology, psychiatry, politics, and theology. Labeling is a way of classifying observable realities. Even the late pastoral psychology specialist Wayne Oates refers to some people in the church as "troublesome." Arthur Paul Boers writes about "difficult" people in congregational life. My experience, research, and observation convince me that for many ministers these terms are too mild. I am writing about people who are more than just troublesome and difficult. I am not trying to demonize normal opposition in church life. But there is a stark fact of life in the ministry: In some churches there is evil, and ministers tend to be the primary victims of it.

The apostle Paul used labels to identify certain church leaders who sought to destroy his ministry ("super-apostles," "false apostles," "deceitful workers," and "his [Satan's] ministers": 2 Cor. 11:5, 13, 15). Jesus labeled Herod a "fox" (Luke 13:32) and called many of the religious leaders of his day "hypocrites" (Matt. 23:13–36). Peter called certain church leaders "false teachers" (2 Peter 2:1), while John referred to one as "evil" (3 John 9–11). I place myself in their tradition and do so from the realm of personal experience.

I will also explain how various factors contribute to clergy abuse, such as passive lay leaders who silently sit on the sidelines and do nothing, letting it happen. Also, autonomous church polity tends to allow abuse by permitting pathological personalities to run roughshod over vulnerable ministers who are not supposed to retaliate or who are left to defend themselves alone.

The wrecking of a minister's life and career will be treated to show the seriousness of ministerial abuse. Abusive persons do considerable damage to the life, welfare, career, and future of the ministers they attack. When a minister is abused and wounded, there is much collateral damage inflicted on the minister's marriage, children, health, peace of mind, as well as his faith, his retirement, and his idealism. Abusers rarely if ever understand, much less care about, the extent of the damage they do to a minister. Other church leaders, who allow this to happen, need to realize the extent and breadth of the damage they permit through their passivity.

Solutions to the Problem

What can be done about this problem? Part 3 of this book will offer concrete suggestions for correction, especially how to get rid of clergy killers, pathological antagonists, and well-intentioned dragons. There are suggestions for godly lay leaders who love their ministers and want to protect them from attack.

Specific steps toward the healing of abused clergy will also be suggested for concerned lay leaders who wish to salvage, heal, and preserve their wounded ministers for a viable and productive future.

What can the wounded minister do for himself? How can he recover from his shattered dreams? How can he listen again to his calling to ministry and recover his original vocation to do God's work in and through the church? Practical ideas will be offered to answer the heartrending needs of the wounded minister.

One thing wounded ministers can do is to become wounded healers for other ministers in pain. Substantive suggestions are offered regarding how to do this over a period of time.

One special chapter is given to a discussion of the other side of this problem, that is, pathological ministers who invite criticism and attack. Churches can be wounded by ministers who are emotionally and/or mentally disturbed. How can these persons be helped? This chapter is only suggestive for much work remains to be done in this area of the church's life and ministry. How can disturbed ministers be identified in advance, before they can damage a church?

Another chapter will be devoted to the problem of church staff associates who are abused by the pastor. A sizeable percentage of ministers who wrote to me or who were interviewed were victims of this type of abuse. This is another sad example of the church, led by the pastor in these instances, shooting its own wounded.

Finally, I will attempt to outline a program of growth for wounded ministers who sincerely want to remain in ministry and grow through and beyond the deep rejection they have experienced. A major purpose of this book is to encourage wounded ministers to recover from their shattered vocational dreams and to find their way back into an active and supportive ministry in the church or in one of its agencies, somewhere, someway, somehow. Another purpose of my writing is to help prevent ministers in service from becoming wounded in the first place. The military issues its personnel bulletproof vests and helmets; what does the church issue for its personnel?

I am well aware that a growing number of ministers are female. Some are senior ministers while many others fill a variety of posts in the ministerial leadership of the church. In most cases, I have tried to remain consistent in my use of masculine pronouns rather than the awkward he/she, him/her, himself/herself. Also, since the great majority of ministers continues to be male, it makes for smoother writing along with easier identification on the part of most readers. Those who abuse clergy also tend to be males, so I have stayed with masculine references, even though some of the most atrocious abusers are women. If this bothers any of my readers, I apologize for this unintended offense.

My desire is that this book be helpful, insightful, redemptive, and preventive for the vast number of wounded ministers in all denominations and the church at large. I also call on the tremendous number of caring, loving, and supportive lay leaders to rise up in defense of their ministers and stop this nonsensical abuse of God's servants. Moreover, this book is my prayer for the healing of all abused clergy.

I want to acknowledge the insights of several researchers and scholars whose works have been extremely helpful to me in writing this book, especially Lloyd Rediger, Kenneth Haugk, M. Scott Peck, Wayne Oates, and Lewis Smedes. Unapologetically I want to acknowledge that they have made my contributions here more credible. I have tried to incorporate their analyses with my own ideas to write a better book of healing for wounded ministers than I could have written without their help. Much has been written on conflict in the church, but little if any that ministers to the pain of wounded ministers. This is the primary focus of this book.

Also, I want to express my appreciation to Mary Suggs, my most competent manuscript editor for Baker Books, for her many helpful suggestions and her literary expertise that has made this a much better and more readable book.

part 1

The Reality of Abuse

1 Clergy Killers on the Loose

The enemy has infiltrated the ranks of the church. These are laypersons who have serious mental or emotional problems and who feel an inner hostility toward clergy-persons. G. Lloyd Rediger of St. Paul, Minnesota, has tagged these individuals "clergy killers."[1] These clergy abusers have one major objective in their role in the church—to abuse or hurt ministers to the degree that they will leave the ministry. Rediger notes:

> Abuse of pastors by congregations and the breakdown of pastors due to inadequate support are now tragic realities. This worst-case scenario for the church, one that is increasing in epidemic proportions, is not a misinterpretation by a few discontented clergy. Rather, it is a phenomenon that is verified by both research and experience.[2]

Notice that Rediger's research convinces him that this is a problem "that is increasing in epidemic proportions." He identifies *clergy killers* as "people who intentionally target pastors for serious injury or destruction."[3]

I have personally experienced abuse at the hands of clergy killers. In addition, I have been listening to the cries for help from numerous other ministers who have struggled through similar experiences. Therefore, I have been gathering stories for some time from a wide variety of clergypersons who have been attacked by clergy killers. Each story is unique yet similar. There are several commonalities among them. However, there is no set pattern or sequence of events that always occurs when a clergy killer is at work. We will look at several common characteristics of this phenomenon.

Common Features in Stories of Abuse

First, each story has a set of problems in the church that serves as background for the conflict that develops between the minister and one or more laypersons who at some point begin identifying the minister as the *cause* of the problems. These problems may include difficulty reaching budget requirements. There may be some kind of intrastaff conflict. Certain key meetings may have been poorly planned. Various volunteer positions in the church have not been filled for some time. The Sunday worship bulletin and weekly mail-out church paper have been poorly organized and printed. A popular staff person has resigned unexpectedly and without explanation. A number of well-known senior adults have complained about being ignored by the church. It does not really matter what the problems are. In most cases the minister is blamed; these people believe he caused the problems. So he is responsible for whatever is wrong in the church and its ministry.

One person seems to start the criticism train rolling. One person takes it on himself to begin pointing out these "serious problems that are hurting our church." Phone calls are made to certain key people. Letters are written, sometimes even unsigned. These complaints all point to one of the church's ministers, usually the senior minister, as the one behind the problems.

Often the person who leads the complaint charge takes several weeks, maybe months, to marshal sympathetic support for his position. Unsuspecting people begin to wonder whether there may be some truth to the complainer's accusations. *I never thought of it like that, but maybe he has a point,* some will reason.

In many cases the initial accuser enlists a few key leaders to plan some meetings to be held at his or a sympathizer's home. These meetings are secret, that is, "invitation only," meetings of people who the accuser believes will agree with his accusations. The primary purpose is to gather support for an eventual attack on their minister. At these meetings, the discussions assist in gathering additional evidence that the minister is to blame for the church's problems. Meticulous notes are usually taken by the accuser or one he designates to do this.

They will try to build a paper trail of accusations with which to charge the minister with inefficiency, poor leadership, lazy work habits, questionable moral behavior, or unchristian attitude. An often-heard complaint is "Oh, it's not so much what he does or says that's so bad; it's the *way* he does or says it." The *way* is never explained; it is just assumed to be bad, unhealthy, conflicting, inappropriate, unkind, or harsh.

The accusing leader plans his attack very carefully. Since he already knows who runs the church, he turns on his charm to win the friendship and support of these people. Those laypersons who run the church are usually an oligarchy (rule of the few) of long-time, recognized leaders who may or may not fill any elected positions in the church organizational structure. They are few in number, and they themselves know who they are. Younger deacons, elders, other elected persons who are young, and new members are rarely a part of this inner leadership core.

The clergy killer knows he must work through recognized authority, this behind-the-scenes oligarchy, to accomplish his goal of getting rid of the minister. When he knows he has their backing, he will move swiftly, with careful calculation.

The attack has actually been going on for some time, but the clergy killer, when the time is right, gets his plan of attack on the agenda of the official board of his church. He arranges for the minister not to be present. The board will be called to "an executive session," meaning no outsiders are invited and that includes the minister. Ministers and their staff members are usually "outsiders" to such official boards. They normally do not vote yet attend regular meetings to make reports on the nature of their work assignments. So it is easy to have a minister excluded from an official board's meeting. He is simply told by the chairman to be somewhere else.

At this crucial meeting, the clergy killer lays his charges before the assembled body of lay leaders. He will use "statistics" to bolster his accusations. A common target is church finances, since most churches never have enough money. The shortage of money can easily be blamed on the minister's leadership. When losing athletic teams see dwindling crowds at games and resultant low game receipts, who tends to get blamed and axed? The coach of course. It's no different in the church. Laypersons tend to think the same in athletics, politics, business, and religion.

Church membership records, attendance figures, the number of conversions and baptisms are all used to measure organizational vitality and are presented to the official board. When the statistics are interpreted negatively, the finger of blame is pointed at the minister. The bottom line of the charges is very simple: If we get rid of our minister, all of our problems will be solved, because we will bring in a new and different minister who will lead us to new heights of statistical glory.

If the accusing leader succeeds to this point, he will probably try to get a special committee appointed (hopefully his friends) to visit the minister in his office as soon as possible to pressure him to resign quietly "for the sake of the church's unity and future." By the time this happens, many ministers have been so harassed and worn out emotionally by all the accusations (via phone calls, letters—some anonymous—personal visits, and rumors) that they will go as quickly and quietly as possible.

This leadership crisis will eventually be brought before the congregation in some official capacity, where it is possible that open conflict will explode. Most ministers have friends and supporters who are caught unawares by the attempt to get rid of them, and these friends will rush to their support if at all possible. It may be too late to prevent the minister's resignation, but some kind of reactive response may take place resulting in either a church split—with some members insisting the resigned minister lead them to start a new congregation—or with the departure of several members in an unorganized fashion to join other churches in town.

At this point, the abused clergyperson usually goes into a clinical depression, after being rejected by the church that called him to be their pastor at one time. His wife and children also feel rejected. They may even stop attending church anywhere for a time. They usually feel some kind of public embarrassment over what happened to their husband and father. The clergyperson's marriage may be severely strained, especially when there are acute financial needs. This "collateral damage" (to be discussed in chapter 7) can be quite heavy and devastating. An already weak or troubled marriage may eventually collapse in separation and divorce, especially if the wife is one who tends to be critical and blames her husband for the problems.

Abused clergy often tell unbelievable stories of turning to their friends in the ministry and to their denominational superiors for help and getting little if any positive assistance. It's as if they now have some dread disease, and their friends, colleagues, and superiors keep their distance. Rarely does anyone come to their aid. If perchance they are recommended by their denomination to another church, the other church may lose interest when they learn that they were fired. Most churches will interpret that as "a problem we don't need." These terminated clergy have to pay their bills, eat, and provide for their families, so they get whatever work they can, sometimes very menial and low-paying jobs, just to survive. Getting a good job isn't easy. What can a minister trained for the ministry do in the secular job market? Not much. This adds to their already chronic depression.

These stories of wounded ministers, abused by churches that allowed one or more clergy killers to get their way, are a sad collection of ministerial tragedies that should never have happened.

Characteristics of Clergy Killers

Who are these clergy killers? What kind of human beings are they? These are not normal people, average complainers, critics, and typical dissidents who are generally unhappy about life itself. Generally there are very few of them, one or two in an average congregation, but they are deadly and have a knack for gathering a following of ordinary folk with common complaints and disagreements in the church. They can easily create the illusion that there are hordes of people against the pastor. They are masters at using the tyrannical *they* in their comments: "*They* are very unhappy about . . ." Or the illusive *people:* "*People* are saying that . . ." These are verbal instruments in the arsenal they use to destroy a minister.

Let me be clear that I am not using the term *clergy killer* to label the person who happens to disagree with a minister and his agenda. Rather, I am using this term to identify persons who have a very mean-spirited disposition toward ministers in general and who intentionally target ministers for termination. Rediger identifies seven characteristics of these vicious people, and my experience confirms this characterization:

1. They are destructive. The damage they want to inflict is intentional and deliberate. They are not out simply to disagree or find fault; they want to inflict pain and damage persons. "Their tactics include sabotage, subverting worthy causes, inciting others to do their dirty work, and causing victims to self-destruct."[4] The clergy killer in my last pastorate used every one of these tactics to accomplish his goals.

2. Clergy killers are determined. They are headstrong and will stop at nothing. They may pause for a time, change strategies, even go underground to reconnoiter, but they will come back with a vengeance to continue their intimidation, networking, and breaking all rules of decency to accomplish their destructive objectives. For them, their plans have priority over all other programs of the church.

3. These persons are deceitful. Clergy killers are masters of manipulation, camouflage, misrepresentation, and accusing others of their own atrocious deeds. Their comments and promises are not trustworthy. They are experts at twisting facts.

4. Clergy killers are demonic. Psychiatrist M. Scott Peck said that there are some people so mean that the only adequate term to describe them is evil.[5] These people in the church who target ministers for destruction may be mentally disordered, but they do not yield to patience or love nor do they honor human decency.

    Apparently clergy killers carry around a lot of internal pain, confusion, anger, and even rage. Spiritual leaders, especially employed parish ministers, become available scapegoats for this pain and confusion, which is unidentified and untreated. Unusual, reactive, and destructive motivations emerge in these disturbed minds. A serious mistake is made, however, when the church and popular culture reject the concept of evil and label clergy-killer behavior as mental illness or human failure. A loss of spiritual understanding of intentional meanness and destruction leaves the church unable to avail itself of the powerful spiritual gifts of discernment, grace, discipline, and courage to confront evil with God's power.

5. Denial on the part of the church leaves clergy killers unrestrained, so that the whole church in general and ministers in particular are left extremely vulnerable to their wiles. The church tends to deny the seriousness of what clergy killers are about and thus unknowingly cooperates in their agenda of destruction. So many in the church, well-intentioned people to be sure, do not wish to admit the reality of clergy killers and the intentional damage they cause. Believing that this evil should not be happening in the church, we convince ourselves that it really isn't happening. Kindhearted church leaders often told me, "Oh, Pastor, this will all blow over. Don't take it so personally. The Lord will take care of this problem if we just keep praying about it."

6. Clergy killers are masters of intimidation, using it to violate the rules of decency and caring that most Christians try to follow. Intimidation is a powerful weapon at a subconscious level, so much so that clergy killers are willing to step up the fight and use tactics that most Christians forbid themselves to use. Actually most clergy are naive when it comes to survival fighting, or what might be called "ecclesiastical street fighting." They do not have the required resources and knowledge of networks in the church for such confrontations. Therefore ministers and their supporters are easily intimidated by these persuasive and charming religious assailants.

7. Clergy killers are experts of disguise when they see it would be to their advantage. They are able to present themselves as pious, devout, and spiritual church members who are doing their destructive work "for the good of the church, to advance God's kingdom." They can convince naive church members that they are raising legitimate issues. These religious monsters often hide among their "allies of opportunity," those members whom they have charmed into friendship—who are also congregational power brokers—and others who are disgruntled with the church for one reason or another.

   Other clergy killers may not choose the strategy of disguising themselves. Rather, they choose to find power in fighting openly. Using bluster, threats, and accusations, they forge ahead with their attacks as if they are unstoppable giants. They openly intimidate any opposition by making it clear they will fight dirty and use any tactic to accomplish their goals. Gentle and peace-at-any-price church members are quickly sidelined by such threats, leaving the ministers and those who support them to cope with the problem the best way they can. Denominational officials can easily fall into this latter category of appeasement, influenced by their desire not to lose the financial support of the congregation whose minister is under fire.

I have observed that a clergy killer who uses disguise at first may come out into the open with his tactics after he has charmed the traditional oligarchy into believing that his cause is just and is for the good of the church.

Clinically speaking, who are clergy killers? What has made them this way? Several possibilities exist. They may possess distinct personality disorders (for example, they may be antisocial, borderline, paranoid, narcissistic). These psychiatric conditions will be discussed in more detail later. It is also possible that clergy killers have been victims of abuse, either in the past or in the present. Inadequate socialization (the process of becoming human), arrested adolescence, or violent role models may be behind their behavior. Some may have a perverse, voyeuristic, and vindictive taste for the suffering of their victims. Others have learned to throw tantrums to get their selfish way. They have learned how to distract, confuse, lie, and seduce to do harm to the vulnerable.

Clergy killers wound or destroy either by direct attacks or by inciting others to inflict the wounds. Sometimes they induce victims to self-destruct by harassing them to the point of frustration and anger. This is the minister who counterattacks angrily from the pulpit. Most congregations will not tolerate for long a minister who expresses angry outbursts during his sermons, however justified he may feel.

Understanding how any person can become a clergy killer is complex and difficult. Most Christians in most churches have never known one, but it takes only one or two in a church to create havoc and bedlam. Because these people live in denial as to their true nature, they would not see themselves in this chapter if they were to read it. Clergy killers have surrounded and insulated themselves with a whole array of defense mechanisms and justifications for their actions. They firmly believe that what they are doing in harming and terminating a minister is the right thing to do. For them, it is the will of God. Nevertheless, they are sick and mean people.

Perpetrators of Church Rage

Sometimes pastors are heard to say, "The meanest people I have ever met are members of a church." Who are they talking about? Clergy killers. These are the perpetrators of church rage who create abusive congregations.

A guest commentary published in a leading denominational journal was entitled, "Baptists Need a Cure for Church Rage." After discussing the problem of road rage, the writer comments:

> Unfortunately, people do not jettison their rage when they come to church. There are no statistics on church rage, but my conversations with pastors and church leaders indicate it is as prevalent as road rage.
>
> There is the tight-fisted layman who seizes a copy of the proposed budget during the business meeting, circles the pastor's salary, tosses the copy of it on the pew and walks out. There are believers who are powerless at work and home, so they wield power in the only arena where they can exercise it—the church. . . . There is the anonymous Unabomber who sends emotionally explosive, unsigned letters.
>
> Sometimes church rage is overt. Tempers flare and voices are raised, often over issues that laid dormant for many years and relate only marginally to church. Most of the time church rage is disguised beneath a veneer of respectability or piousity [sic].
>
> Most church rage, unfortunately, is unleashed with such casual indifference or unrestrained glee that it bears little resemblance to the compassionate indignation displayed by Jesus. Neither does it look much like the fruit of the Spirit—love, joy, peace, patience, kindness, goodness, faithfulness, gentleness and self-control—most of which act strongly like an antidote to church rage.

The fruit of the Spirit plus the grace of Christ is more apt to produce compassionate tears than brittle and destructive rage. True prophets weep more than they seethe.[6]

In another issue of this denominational journal, Ken Coffee, an associate director of the Texas Baptist State Missions Commission, describes abusive congregations:

A deacon chairman tells of being accosted by an irate church member in the halls of the church. "She stuck her finger in my face and said, 'If you can't straighten out that preacher then we will just have to do it for you.' She wasn't just talking. She was screaming at the top of her voice. Her face was red and the veins in her forehead were protruding so much I thought they would burst."

There are a number of churches in which this kind of abusive behavior has been long-standing. No one seems to know exactly when it began. It has continued in some churches through numerous leadership changes. In some churches it has come to the point that deacons refuse to serve as chairman and prospective pastors are frightened off by stories of the treatment of former pastors.[7]

One pastor wrote to me the following: "In my first pastorate, I had two elderly deacons who expressed opposition to the church on the issue concerning the ordination of certain divorced men to the deacon ministry. The church had surveyed the members and asked them to pray about the matter. They knew these men and their good reputations in the community. Most of the members were in favor of the ordination. But these two older men had run the church because the previous pastor was bivocational and lived away from the town. They were used to growling and getting their way.

"At a called deacons' meeting, I was cursed and denounced by the eldest of the two for following through with the ordination. He would have nothing to do with it, except that I tell the church to change its mind, and then I was to resign. The deacon body was pretty much evenly divided over the issue, and I did not feel led to back down. The other elderly deacon said he would go along with the church if he could hear the sordid details of the men's previous marriages.

"One of these deacons began a smear campaign on my character and accused me of lewd behavior, of all things, in the pulpit. My wife's and daughters' reputations were slandered by this man. He went so far as to call the district denominational executive to cast a shadow over my reputation as a minister. It was a very trying time for my family and me.

"In my next pastorate, I ran into a situation of another deacon-controlled church. The deacon body wished to ordain a man because he was a 'good ol' boy' and was younger than sixty. The man had a temper and was emotionally unstable. This was common knowledge to the town and most of the members of the church. I pleaded with the chairman of deacons not to follow through with this man's ordination, but to no avail.

"This man was ordained and proved to be a real harm to the fellowship. On one occasion, he became angry at a seventy-year-old woman who was making copies at the church office. He stormed into the copy room and began to shout and curse her for meddling in his business. She had earlier expressed a concern about his health to the man's wife, whom she saw at the local bank. The wife had told him about it. He was furious, but I managed to get between them and allowed the elderly lady to escape the room to safety.

"The man's anger was then vented on me, and threats were made to me. The only advantage I had was size and I was able to steer him to the door and out of the building. He left the parking lot shouting insults and threats all the way. When I later told the deacon leaders about this, they just laughed it off, accusing me of exaggeration. This unstable man continued to cause such trouble that I simply resigned in disgust and moved to another church."

The reader may be thinking that such behavior is so rare and bizarre that it is hardly worth mentioning. I wish that were so. It certainly doesn't happen every day or every week in most churches, but these kinds of stories from wounded ministers have turned up with such regularity in my correspondence files that I believe they happen more often than we might think. Clergy killers exist in greater numbers than we are willing to admit.

Abusive congregations and church rage are signs of clergy killers at work. These are sick and mean people tolerated by sick and weak churches. The victims are the ministers.

2

Pathological Antagonists in the Church

While serving as the pastor of a promising congregation, located in a strategic area of rapid growth in a major metropolitan city, I ran head-on into extremely stiff opposition from a small group of lay leaders. Certain men, whose intransigent spirits and antagonistic dispositions I had never observed before in over forty years of ministry, led the attack. It was during my second and third years of ministry there that my primary antagonist launched a crusade. Beginning with anonymous notes to me, followed by signed letters to the church's deacons and other leaders, he accused me of all sorts of outright erroneous and ridiculous charges. This was not logical or reasonable opposition based on mere differences of opinion. It was meanness, pure and simple. This man could be persuasive, charming, and persistent. He was also often mean-spirited and hateful. I needed help understanding him.

This was when I discovered the work of Kenneth Haugk, minister and clinical psycholological in St. Louis, Missouri. This chapter is a presentation of what I learned from Haugk's careful analysis of antagonism in the church, coupled with my own interpretations.

Clergy abusers can be either identified with or supported by what some psychologists call pathological antagonists. Haugk defines antagonists as "individuals who, on the basis of nonsubstantive evidence, go out of their way to make insatiable demands, usually attacking the person or performance of others. These attacks

35

are selfish in nature, tearing down rather than building up, and are frequently directed against those in a leadership capacity."[1]

Clergy abusers are pathological antagonists who need to be understood. They are pathological because their attitude and behavior are abnormal, that is, characteristic of disease.

What Is a Pathological Antagonist?

Antagonism is the stimulus of a major disruption in a church caused by the mean-spirited attitude and behavior of an antagonist. *Antagonism* is usually defined as actively expressed opposition, hostility, or antipathy. Haugk's description of an antagonist when combined with Rediger's depiction of a clergy killer is helpful in understanding this kind of upheaval in a congregation. I have observed firsthand the following characteristics of a pathological antagonist:

1. The arguments of a pathological antagonist are usually founded on little or terribly misrepresented evidence. Some common logical fallacies employed are *pettifogging* (quibbling over petty details, offering strong proof of irrelevant points); *extension* (exaggerating the position of one's opponent); *argumentum ad ignoratium* (making an accusation that cannot be disproved and then claiming that this makes it true).[2] From my experience with a clergy killer, I would add another fallacy—outright *lying or falsification*. An antagonist, in his attempt to make the kill, will take certain facts and so twist them that they are blatantly false when presented. In time he convinces himself that his twisted facts are true.

2. I have often observed that a pathological antagonist will initiate trouble. This person is hypersensitive to any word or action, even trivial oversights, so that he takes these things as a personal attack and responds aggressively. Failing to speak to him in the hall, not asking him to pray at meetings, not getting his approval in advance for an idea you wish to propose to the church, or not recognizing him sufficiently before the congregation are examples of behavior that will

cause his antagonism to flare up. He will take these as evidence that you are against him.

3. It became clear to me that the pathological antagonist is never satisfied. His demands are insatiable. No amount of accommodation on the minister's part will ever suffice. Attempts at appeasement will not calm him down but will encourage him to make more demands. This person will fight on until there is nothing left but debris. He is persistent and unstoppable.

4. The pathological antagonist will lead a campaign of attack on the minister. This person is not trying to give constructive criticism. Even if some valid points are offered, his goal is nothing short of control, no matter what it may cost the minister or the church. The antagonist is so full of rage that he feels compelled to attack the "enemy" (the minister) until he is destroyed (terminated and eliminated from the scene).

   This person probably has a "God-problem." He feels some deep-seated anger toward God, for some reason out of his past experiences. Because it is difficult to show anger directly toward God, the pathological antagonist chooses the minister, the "man of God," as his target. Sometimes this anger is guilt-driven (possibly due to some hidden sin, such as an extramarital affair, for example). His antagonism is an attempt to move the spotlight off his own sins and onto another. Therefore the attack is a smoke screen to cover his own moral indiscretions.

5. It was obvious to me that the attacking behavior of the pathological antagonist is selfish in nature. Often he will seize on some spiritual goal or objective, such as the good of the church and its work in the community, and pretend this is what he is fighting for. This person is rarely interested in authentic spiritual goals. If one rationale no longer works to his advantage, he will devise another, such as keeping the young people from leaving the church. His stated reasons for opposition are a ruse for his own hidden agenda. What he really wants is power, control, status, and authority.

6. The attacks of the pathological antagonist are for destruction rather than construction. The antagonist's actions divide the church; they do not pull the people together. My expe-

rience concurs with Haugk when he writes, "Show me a divided and strife-torn congregation, and I will show you a congregation that has one or more antagonists in its midst."[3]

Types of Pathological Antagonists

Pathological antagonists are not of one kind. Haugk helps us distinguish between three different types.[4]

Hard-Core Antagonists

Hard-core antagonists are seriously disturbed people, even psychotic, that is, out of touch with reality. Their psychosis is of the paranoid type, which is not easy to detect. These people can appear normal either some or most of the time. They have incredible persistence and an extreme desire to make trouble, even enjoying their sadistic inclinations. One can easily spot one of these individuals by the smirk often seen on his face, especially noticeable after he makes a critical or snide remark about the pastor in a meeting of church leaders.

Hard-core antagonists are identical to Rediger's "clergy killer" types. They will go to any length and expense to wreak havoc on their targets. As far as they are concerned, they are fighting a jihad, a holy war, and the minister is the enemy. They believe they are doing God a favor. Their inner rage is baptized in the aura of holy zeal. Without a doubt, the hard-core antagonist is slippery and dangerous. He cannot be reasoned with.

The apostle Paul may have had this kind of people in mind when he warned the Ephesian elders about "savage wolves" infiltrating the congregation and "not sparing the flock" (Acts 20:28–29).

Major Antagonists

Most major antagonists are not as severely disturbed as the hard-core ones, but they will at times demonstrate similar behaviors. If the hard-core antagonist *cannot* be reasoned with because of emotional instability, the major antagonist *refuses* to be reasoned with.

Reason is within his capacity, but he knows that if he uses it, he may be defeated or proved wrong. So to protect his position, he simply refuses to be reasonable and his demands are insatiable.

This individual probably has a character or personality disorder seen in the heavy load of anger he carries about together with an overwhelming lust for power. He is not psychotic or out of touch with reality, but his personality problems are obviously deep-seated. A major antagonist does not want to change, since change is threatening to him. He has built a defensive wall around himself, labeled "I am right; what I am doing is right."

Moderate Antagonists

Moderate antagonists lack the self-starting quality of the first two types, who would intentionally give a minister trouble. The moderate antagonist initiates trouble only if the opportunity presents itself—however, he will quickly follow a hard-core or a major antagonist in causing trouble—but he lacks the perseverance of the other two. He has personality problems, but they are not as severe as those of the hard-core or the major types.

Well-Intentioned Dragons

The second and third types above may approximate what Marshall Shelley calls "well-intentioned dragons." Their goals may allegedly be the best interests of the church, but their methods and attitudes are still those of a dragon, doing more harm than good, undermining the ministry of the church without intending to do so.[5]

All three of the above types are malevolent in both intent and effect. I am distinguishing here somewhat between degrees of meanness. These types are different from those we call *activists*, who are devoted to a worthy cause or who push for constructive change in a group's way of thinking or acting. Activists are committed to an issue such as a world hunger offering or a building program or an antiabortion crusade; they really care about something important to them. But they are issue-oriented, not person-centered as the pathological antagonists are.

Certainly all of us act antagonistically at times, acting out of character, selfishly, destructively, maybe even maliciously. But isolated antagonistic behaviors do not make a person a pathological antagonist. Pathological antagonists possess an insatiable desire to drag problems out interminably, eventually wearing down the target of opposition. Pathological antagonists precipitate conflict that is unhealthy and destructive. It is important to note that not all conflict is of this character. Some conflicts can be both healthy and constructive.[6]

Displaced Antagonism

As a pastor, I could not understand why some few individuals were so antagonistic. Most of the people were not of this disposition. And why was one antagonist so negative and critical in every meeting he attended? When I learned from a close friend of his that he had been involved in some indiscreet behavior in the not-too-distant past, I reasoned that he was subconsciously trying to cover up his guilt by focusing all of the attention on my leadership "blunders." I was the sinner and the cause of all of the church's problems, while he was the saint, trying to save the church from decline and failure, even though our growth statistics proved there was no danger of failure.

Then I learned that when he had joined our church three years before I became the pastor, he and his wife came from a denomination known for its legalistic and intransigent ideology and morality. His views reflected the attitude of those who are quick to point out others' faults and shortcomings. The church he came from is well-known for its judgmental attitude toward those with whom they disagree. So it made sense that he simply brought his legalistic background with him into our church.

Another thing I learned about this man as time went by was that he came out of a family that was extremely judgmental. Although I never met his father, I was told by close friends of the family that he was a very controlling and dictatorial man. I got to know his mother. She would write me hateful letters insisting that I resign if I could not be a better pastor. Her criticisms were either very picky about trivial details (for example, mistakes in the worship bulletin) or were so general in nature, there would be no way of responding (for example, my sermons "were not meeting the needs of the people"). This woman was a very cantankerous widow whose entire life was one long story of unhappiness. I suspected that this attitude had rubbed off on her son. I doubt that he had ever been unconditionally loved by his parents and had ever been taught how to love other people. He was angry partly because he had never experienced any meaningful love in his own life.

One antagonist was a retired military man. After his retirement he tried his hand at several types of business ventures. Every single one of them had been a miserable failure. Over the years I had noticed that persons who tended to be failures in their chosen careers were inclined to come into the church and take key leadership roles while exercising a strong controlling modus operandi. Their reasoning seemed to be that, although they were failures outside the church, they could be somebody important in the church. When this man sought and secured several different key positions in our church, this appeared to be sort of an overkill to prove his point that he was a "Mister Big."

Pathological antagonists appear to display the defense mechanism of displacement whereby the focus of their antagonism is shifted from the person(s) or situation that first evoked their negative feelings to someone else or some other group. This happens because the antagonist finds it difficult or impossible, for whatever reasons, to direct his antagonism toward the original cause (which could be God, a parent, a spouse, a sibling, poor health, or job failures, among other things). I once saw a cartoon that illustrated displacement with a series of frames: In succession, a man was severely rebuked by his employer; the man goes home and lambastes his wife; the wife in turn berates her son, who goes outside and kicks the dog.

Pathological antagonists often have a serious God-problem. I recall one person who had failing health. At only age fifty he could not work. His wife had to carry the load of the family financially. He felt humiliated that due to his poor health he was unable to be the primary breadwinner of the family. So he did what many people do: He blamed God. Since he had neither the means nor the courage to attack God, he subconsciously attacked the one who most publicly represents God, the "man of God," his pastor, a safe target for the inner rage he felt toward God. People like this operate out of a core belief: "You hurt me, so I'll hurt you." This is the tactic of revenge. While some persons get depressed, antagonists get even.

In the church the pathological antagonist displaces his anger and hostile actions onto those people who are easy, available, and vulnerable targets for his venom. A minister is a logical choice for such attacks. The target is not the cause of his antagonism but is simply the receiver of it. The minister is the unfortunate victim of the antagonist's attacks.

The Followers of Pathological Antagonists

A pathological antagonist tends to attract certain followers. Without them, the antagonist's efforts would fizzle. He usually does not have the courage to go it alone. He needs followers to bolster his campaign against the minister. My antagonist was calculating in his enlistment of a small band of followers. Each had a personal ax to grind with regard to what was happening in the church. Each had a reputation of being a severe critic of former ministers. All but one was a natural follower in personality makeup.

Jack, the antagonist, was smart. He knew who was the unofficial head of the church, a man who was also a military retiree who had been the recognized lay leader of the church for many years. Deacon Jim controlled the church finances by serving as the perennial chairman of the finance committee. Even when he was supposed to rotate off the committee (according to the church committee manual), he always managed to stay on the committee as chairman. This was important since it was his primary power base for controlling the church. The passive nature of the other church leaders simply allowed this to happen. With his charm, Jack gradually convinced Jim to join him in his attacks on me. I later learned that Jack spent an inordinate amount of time at Jim's home and on the telephone with him, making his case for my termination "in order to save the church."

Four others were enlisted to join in this effort. They began to hold secret meetings at Jim's home on Wednesday evenings (at the same time the congregation was scheduled to hold midweek prayer meetings at the church building). So Jack won over five men and their wives to concur with his accusations, none of which was true. All of these men were deacons. Then, one by one, a few of their longtime friends, nondeacons, were persuaded to see things at church their way.

In a few months, they knew they could count on at least 30 church members to vote with them regarding the minister's future. In the final showdown business meeting, they were able to muster some 50 members to vote with them. There were some 135 members who voted to sustain the minister. These were not good odds for future unity and fellowship in the church. Therefore, I chose to take early retirement. My health was too fragile to continue living with this kind of stress.

Now why would a handful of malcontents, led by a pathological antagonist, be able to enlist followers in a crusade based on a combination of falsehoods and half-truths? Again, Kenneth Haugk helps us. He suggests the following reasons why some individuals follow antagonists:

- People may mistake an antagonist for an activist.
- Truth is often far less exciting than lies and half-truths.
- Bad news is more thrilling than good news.
- Some folks are gullible and naive, and an antagonist will take full advantage of that.
- Some folks are prone to follow orders without question.
- Some shy persons are easily intimidated by an antagonist.
- There are always those passive people who don't want to rock the boat.
- Some unhappy people will follow an antagonist to be one of the crowd.
- Some folks will join an antagonist as a way of expressing their own negative feelings.
- Some individuals will follow an antagonist because of misguided loyalties. (Ministers eventually leave, but these friends will always be here, they reason.)
- Others may follow an antagonist because antagonists sometimes make their followers feel important (especially when the antagonist is a charmer).[7]

Using Haugk's typology, the followers of pathological antagonists seem to resemble the "moderate antagonists." Many people have a tendency to follow powerful and influential leaders, but those who actively follow and support pathological antagonists allow their follower tendency to blind them to the realities of the situation. We must not forget that even Adolf Hitler had the active support of many well-intentioned but naive religious leaders in Germany in the early days of his dictatorship.

Biblical Precedents

The role, danger, and possibility of antagonists in a church are nothing new in Christian history. Even in the Bible, examples may be found. There is the classic precedent of Judas Iscariot who sought vigorously to deter Jesus from his primary mission. Even Judas realized the power value of being the treasurer of the disciples, just as Jack my antagonist had learned. A pathological antagonist will always betray the divine mission of the church even "in the name of God." Jack often invoked the name of God to justify his behavior to eliminate the minister from office. Betrayal comes in many shapes and sizes. The biblical explanation is that "Satan entered into Judas called Iscariot" (Luke 22:3). It is not incidental that the basic meaning of *Satan* is "accuser," which is the primary role of an antagonist.

There is also the precedent of the apostle Paul's antagonists at Corinth who are unnamed but were very distracting to his ministry. The actions of these persons, who are often identified by scholars as legalistic Judaizers, serve as the background for chapters 10–13 of 2 Corinthians. These antagonists infiltrated the church and sought to discredit Paul's message and ministry. He referred to them as "super-apostles" (11:5; see also 12:11), having just suggested that their work seemed patterned after the work of the deceptive serpent in the Garden of Eden, the results of which would be to lead their thoughts away "from a sincere and pure devotion to Christ" (11:3). This deception is called a "different spirit" and a "different gospel" from that received through Paul's ministry (11:4). The antagonists' message is of "another Jesus than the one we proclaimed" (11:4).

Moreover, Paul calls these boasting antagonists "false apostles, deceitful workers, disguising themselves as apostles of Christ." Then he directly identifies them as ministers of Satan who disguise themselves as angels of light and ministers of righteousness but falsely so (11:13–15). In a spirit of stern judgment, the apostle states, "Their end will match their deeds" (11:15). He goes on to observe that these antagonists have made slaves of the Corinthian believers, preyed upon them, taken advantage of them, put on airs, and given them a slap in the face (11:20). Paul even chides the Corinthian saints for not having commended (defended) him in the face of these antagonists (12:11).

In addition, Paul is fearful that when he returns to Corinth, he will find the church embroiled in "quarreling, jealousy, anger, self-ishness, slander, gossip, conceit, and disorder" (12:20) as a consequence of their having followed and supported these antagonists. Paul implies that his ministry had been for "building up and not for tearing down" (13:10), an implication that the work of the antagonists had been for tearing down. He concludes by appealing to his readers to live together in agreement and peace with the promise that "the God of love and peace will be with you" (13:11).

Another biblical precedent of antagonism is the case of Diotrephes mentioned in the apostle John's third letter. John characterizes this antagonist as one "who likes to put himself first" and "does not acknowledge our authority" (v. 9). John accuses Diotrephes of "spreading false charges against us. And not content with those charges, he refuses to welcome the friends [fellow believers], and even prevents those who want to do so and expels them from the church" (v. 10). John then concludes with the appeal: "Beloved, do not imitate what is evil but imitate what is good. Whoever does good is from God; whoever does evil has not seen God" (v. 11).

Those of us in ministry who have dealt with pathological antagonists could not find a more descriptive portrayal of their evil work than John's. Arrogant, harsh, cruel, caustically critical, unloving, unkind, deceptive, disruptive, and divisive, these persons are clearly not of God. As one of my lay leader supporters said to me, "These men are like a cancerous tumor in one's body; the only way to deal with it is surgery."

3 When Evil Invades the Church

One of the hardest lessons I had to learn in the ministry was that evil can invade a church. As the apostle Peter warned, "Discipline yourselves, keep alert. Like a roaring lion your adversary the devil prowls around, looking for someone to devour" (1 Peter 5:8). It never occurred to me that Satan could do his prowling around in a church, nor that it would be the minister he would try to devour. I had spent the first eighteen years of my life in a church where nothing like this had ever happened. The next forty-two years of my ministry were a mix of victories and setbacks, with more positives than negatives. But in my sixtieth year I discovered that it can in fact happen; the devil will use certain persons to try to devour the minister.

The warnings of Paul in Romans 16:17–20 began to have a loud ring of reality:

> I urge you, brothers and sisters, to keep an eye on those who cause dissensions and offenses, in opposition to the teaching that you have learned; avoid them. For such people do not serve our Lord Christ, but their own appetites, and by smooth talk and flattery they deceive the hearts of the simple-minded. . . . I want you to be wise in what is good and guileless in what is evil. The God of peace will shortly crush Satan under your feet.

If evil could invade the early church, it can do so today. Writing out of my own experience, I do not wish to sound harsh or bitter, but I do feel compelled to be realistic about what can happen in a church. When a congregation is naive to the deceptiveness of Satan and will passively allow a small group of clergy abusers to beat up their pastor, there is deep trouble in the church. Lloyd Rediger perceptively notes:

> It is the growing presence of incivility and abuse in the church that has become the greatest source of confusion, pain, and injustice for pastors. To dislike and criticize a pastor is not uncommon and might even be understandable. But abusing pastors mentally, spiritually, and physically is now a clergy nightmare come true. The growing abuse is also a significant commentary on the mental and spiritual health of the church, for how the church treats its leaders reveals even more about the church than about its leaders. *Only a sick or dying church batters its pastors.*[1]

I am not discussing here the normal give-and-take of church conflict, which sometimes can become what Ron Susek calls a "firestorm."[2] There is considerable difference between normal church conflict—which Susek observes moves through recognizable phases—and an evil force led by mean-spirited pathological antagonists who plan and work for the destruction of the leader's ministry. The former is to be expected among humans, while the latter is evil, aberrant behavior. This raises the question of how a church can allow itself to become an instrument of evil, attacking its own spiritual leader.

The Reality of Evil Today

The Bible isn't the only source of warning about evil in today's world. The field of psychiatry has its contemporary prophets alerting us to this demonic reality. Psychiatrist M. Scott Peck notes that certain forms of behavior can only be described as *evil*. His writings have been widely recognized in recent years as tremendously perceptive regarding the shadow side of human nature.

In his first major work, *The Road Less Traveled,* Peck, not a Christian at the time of its writing, outlined his personal search for and observations regarding what he called "spiritual growth."[3] After his conversion to Christianity, he wrote about the nature of evil in *The People of the Lie*. Both of these books have been extremely helpful, especially to ministers. After reading Peck, I came to several conclusions about many of the struggles we ministers have in the church. Much of what follows is an attempt to marshal the support of one of America's leading psychiatrists to affirm that evil is a pathological reality in the life of many local churches. These are my conclusions based on Peck's insights.

In the Church

First, I pull no punches about the insidious and deceptive nature of evil in the arena of religion, not only in organized religion but also in a "baptized" culture. Some of the most atrocious expressions of evil hide under the umbrella of religion. Any astute student of both secular and church history over these past two thousand years knows this. Consequently, ministers should not be surprised when evil shows its ugly head in their church, for example, when a deacon or other church member launches an unjustified attack on the minister's reputation, ability, or character to the degree that serious damage is the ultimate goal of such an attack.

A Personality Disorder

Evil is not merely a biblical way of describing certain forms of mental illness. Although Peck does not consider evil persons "ill," he is concerned that traditional psychiatry does not have a category designating evil persons as evil. Psychiatry believes that naming a pathological condition is important in treating it. Peck agrees and states:

> The time is right, I believe, for psychiatry to recognize a distinct new type of personality disorder to encompass those I have named evil. In addition to the abrogation of responsibility that characterizes all personality disorders, this one would specifically be distinguished by:
>
> (a) consistent destructive, scapegoating behavior, which may often be quite subtle.

(b) excessive, albeit usually covert, intolerance to criticism and other forms of narcissistic injury.

(c) pronounced concern with a public image and self-image of respectability, contributing to a stability of life-style but also to pretentiousness and denial of hateful feelings or vengeful motives.

(d) intellectual deviousness, with an increased likelihood of a mild schizophreniclike disturbance of thinking at times of stress.[4]

Therefore, identifying certain persons as "evil" is not simply demonizing one's opponents, but recognizing that behavior that seeks to damage another intentionally is more than merely "a difference of opinion"; it is evil. In some cases, the commitment to do harm, to tear down, to destroy could be seen as just short of murder, because the evil actions are intended to kill the leader's ministry, career, position in the church, and even his health. Apparently there are no pricks of conscience at all. Rather, the perpetrator feels fully justified.

The Effects of Evil

Evil may be defined as that which is in opposition to life. It was Peck's eight-year-old son who put it simply, "Why, Daddy, evil is 'live' spelled backward." Evil is about killing, destruction, and harm, even killing the spirit. This applies to the actions of a clergy killer who is a master at destroying the spirit of a minister, possibly driving him from the ministry. Pathological antagonists can also effectively destroy the spirit of a church, disrupting its fellowship, dividing the congregation into camps, harassing its minister out of the pulpit, arresting its growth, even destroying its future.

Cloaked by the Ordinary

Evil persons are good at cloaking their evil nature and intentions. They often finagle their way into places of leadership in the church whereby they gain credibility and authority in the eyes of the congregation at large. Once in positions of power, they will move to disrupt, control, and discredit the recognized ministerial leadership already in place. We tend to think that evil people will always be little Adolf Hitlers trying to dominate and ruin. Yet real evil may show itself where you least expect it—in the clerk in the neighborhood store or the lay leader in the church down the street. My own experience convinced me that evil persons are quite common and may appear quite ordinary to the casual observer.

Consistency of Evil

There is a difference between evil and "ordinary" sin. It is not individual sins as such that characterize evil people but the subtlety, persistence, and consistency of their sins. The central defect of evil persons is not their sin but their refusal to acknowledge it. Pathological antagonists look very much like other members of the congregation. They can pray pious prayers and talk the language of the church. They can teach Sunday school, serve on committees, and sing hymns. They can sound very sincere and "spiritual." Their evil actions are so subtle and covert that they cannot clearly be designated as crimes.

Criminals in prison are more likely to be open and honest about their crimes. They even call themselves the "honest criminals." They tell us that the truly evil people live in the free world. Although self-justifying, these claims are often accurate. Most people in prison can be classified by a standard psychiatric diagnosis of one sort or another, ranging, in layman's terms, from crazy to impulsive to aggressive to an absence of conscience. Clergy killers and pathological antagonists in the church have no such obvious defects and do not fall into any standard psychiatric classification. This is not because these people are healthy but because psychiatry has not developed a definition of their aberration.

Moreover, we need to distinguish between evil as a basic personality characteristic and evil deeds. Evil actions do not make a person evil. If that were so, then all of us would be evil. Sin is a violation of the will of God, a breaking of God's commandments, a deviation from his law, or failure to do something we ought to have done. So all of us are sinners. Yet our sins are random, inconsistent, occasional. On the other hand, evil persons' sins are consistent; their destructiveness is both subtle and unrelenting. They deny their own sinfulness. They are intransigent, refusing to change because they do not believe they need to change. They are the truly self-righteous; they can do no wrong; they have no sin. Calls for them to repent fall on deaf ears because they believe there is nothing in their behavior of which to repent. They do not change because they will not; they feel there is no reason to change.

Evil persons attack others rather than face their own faults. They are masters of scapegoating. Everything wrong is someone else's fault. They refuse to grow spiritually because such growth would require them to admit they need to grow. Therefore, they must eliminate the evidence of their imperfections, and they do this primarily by projecting their own evil deeds on others, usually those in authority. Rarely does a pathological antagonist go after another member of the church; no, he must go after the minister. By destroying the "man of God," the antagonist elevates himself to the high throne of virtue and perfection. Yet instead of destroying others, antagonists should be destroying the evil sickness within themselves.

Without Conscience

Evil persons are usually people without a conscience. Some may fit the description of what psychiatrists call psychopaths or sociopaths. They not only do harm, but do so with reckless abandon. But a pathological antagonist is a different sort of evil person: He is self-righteous and dedicated to preserving his self-image of perfection. Pathological antagonists worry about maintaining the appearance of moral goodness or purity. They are very sensitive to what others think of them. They dress well, go to work on time, pay taxes, and outwardly live lives that are above reproach, although they may have skeletons in their closets from the past. Their goodness, however, is all on the level of pretense. In effect, it is a lie.

The absence of a conscience is actually a conscience covered over with numerous rationalizations or self-justifications. Pathological antagonists are unwilling to tolerate a sense of sin or imperfection. Subconsciously they are aware of their evil nature and actions but are desperately trying to avoid being aware of their evil. They tend to be involved in a major cover-up. This is not a defective conscience but a denial of the conscience's warnings. They become evil by attempting to hide from themselves. The wickedness of evil persons is found in the cover-up process. As Peck notes, "Evil originates not in the absence of guilt but in the effort to escape it."[5]

Evil persons are masters of disguise, of cover-up. I well recall one antagonist at various church meetings wearing a smirky grin hiding his hatred, exhibiting his smooth and oily manner that masked his fury, wearing, as it were, a velvet glove that covered a fist. But he was such an expert at disguise that it was seldom possible to pinpoint the maliciousness of his evil. His disguise was often impenetrable. However, there were times we could catch glimpses of his uncanny game of hide-and-seek, as he evaded, avoided, and hid from himself. This man was in intense pain, a pain he could not tolerate—the pain of his own battered and aching conscience reminding him, however subtly, of his own sinfulness, meanness, and imperfection.

I suggested to one antagonist during my last week as his pastor that he seek psychotherapy. He was furious at my suggestion. He would do anything to avoid the pain of self-examination. Evil persons hate the light of goodness that reveals their true nature, the light of scrutiny that would expose their sins, and the light of truth that would expose their deceptiveness. The last place we would ever find an evil person would be in a therapist's office. Undergoing self-observation would seem to him like suicide. Peck observes, "The most significant reason we know so little scientifically about human evil is simply that the evil are so extremely reluctant to be studied."[6]

Self-Centered and Arrogant

Evil persons are extremely self-centered and arrogant. They allegedly have all the answers. It appears that the central defect of evil persons is a special strain of narcissism.

Psychiatry's description of a narcissistic personality disorder includes grandiosity, self-centeredness, emotional isolation, and manipulativeness. There is an exaggerated sense of self-importance and grandiose fantasies marked by idealization. Exhibitionism and lack of empathy also characterize the narcissistic personality disorder. The affect is turbulent, fluctuating between indifference, rage, shame, humiliation, and empty boredom. Interpersonal relationships are disrupted constantly by excessive exploitiveness, inconsideration, and an alternating pattern of overidealization and devaluation of those who are close.[7]

One antagonist I knew was the best example of narcissism and a narcissistic personality disorder I have ever seen. He fit all of the above descriptions.

While to some degree mentally healthy persons submit themselves to their own conscience, evil persons exhibit an unusual willfulness. These people are determined to have their own way at any cost, especially to other people. They have extraordinary power in their attempts to control others. Evil always seeks to control others, which leads to the destruction of those being controlled. This can be observed both in individuals and in small groups that take over a local congregation or an entire denomination of churches. The takeover is always achieved through manipulative measures. The willfulness of control is at the heart of evil behavior. Peck observes, "The strong will—the power and authority—of Jesus radiates from the Gospels, just as Hitler's did from *Mein Kampf*. But Jesus' will was that of his Father, and Hitler's that of his own. The crucial distinction is between 'willingness and willfulness'" (quoting Gerald G. May, *Will and Spirit*).[8]

Churches simply must heed Peck's insights if they are ever going to stop wounding their ministers.

How Does Evil Penetrate a Church?

If evil is so terrible, how does it penetrate the structure and life of a church, of all places? The church is the people of God, the household of faith, the body of Christ, the communion of the Holy Spirit. Is evil stronger than God and his people? How can Satan get inside a church and cause so much trouble? Let's look at several answers to these questions.

Naïveté of Church People

It seems that, unfortunately, most church folk are extremely naive about the nature of evil in the world today. The reason for the above lengthy section is to inform the church and its leaders, both lay and ordained, about the reality of this demonic force. The average lay person simply does not understand the nature and power of "the wiles of the devil" (Eph. 6:11). The apostle Paul warns us about this problem. So serious is it that he calls on believers to "put on the whole armor of God" to engage in this battle (Eph. 6:10–20). He does not say that the battle is *outside* the church but implies that it can be anywhere the people of God are functioning, yes, even *inside* the church.

Over a period of a few months, I saw one antagonist navigate his way into several key positions in the church. No one opposed his election to any of these positions, except in one instance: One woman who knew his background (especially regarding his indiscreet behavior of several months previous to this time) during the nominating committee's discussion of him spoke up in opposition to his being chosen as a church officer. She did not state her true reasons for opposing him, only that she thought it would be unwise to nominate him. The other members of the committee overruled her and presented his name to the church. As a member of the nominating committee, this person had volunteered for the position. Most of the people could not believe that this very active member would or could be a problem to anyone. At that time, none of us saw him as a pathological antagonist who would become a major disruptive force in the life of the congregation.

Preoccupied with Maintenance

I have observed that when a church is more concerned with its internal operations, with "maintenance" of the organization, than it is with ministry, it becomes vulnerable to attempts at internal political control of the organization. When a church is focused on taking care of itself, paying off its mortgage, paying its bills, and saving money, and shows little interest in outreach, evangelism, ministry, and missions, it is often headed for trouble. Churches that are more committed to winning new converts and discipling them in the faith than to questions of "Who's in charge here?" have their priorities in order and will be less vulnerable to Satan's attacks. Outreach, evangelism, ministry, and missions will keep a congregation on its knees in prayer (which always frightens Satan away). Satan can more easily invade a church that is consumed with secondary matters.

Elevating Administration

Evil can better penetrate a church when its leaders have developed an administrative philosophy rather than a ministry role. Administration is a necessary part of directing a church's life, but administration must always be a means and never an end. When deacons and other lay leaders see themselves primarily as administrators, then control is likely to be more important than ministry. When deacons emphasize that they are a "board" (not a biblical concept), or when elders call themselves "ruling elders," watch out. Control will become the primary issue.

Because one antagonist had previously been a member of a denomination where the local church is divided into ruling elders and teaching elders, he sought to influence our deacons to function as ruling elders, which was not advocated in our church's organization and polity. Even though our deacon chairman kept reminding the deacon body that their role was ministry and not administration, this antagonist was able to persuade a small number of them that they were in fact ruling elders, even the bosses of the minister. The silent majority passively allowed this to happen. I was subsequently stripped of any authority and relegated to the role of a chaplain to those who ran the church. Because I would not agree to this unbiblical concept of the minister, I became a target for termination.

A Philosophy of Appeasement

When the good, prayerful, dedicated, loving lay leaders are afraid of conflict in the church and have no stomach for challenging those who are using secular political methods to run the church, they will choose a philosophy of appeasement rather than reasonable confrontation. Evil will then take advantage of what appears to be an open door to take over and control the church.

Jack the antagonist enlisted five others to support his campaign to force the minister to resign. Together they wrote letters (although Jack composed them himself) containing blatant lies and half-truths about the minister and sent them to the other deacons and numerous other church members. Numerous telephone calls were made to spread their venom. There was no love or compassion in what they said. It was organized meanness. Pleas for help from the minister to those not involved in the campaign of hate were met with unbelief that there were any evil intentions to get rid of the minister. They were typical of people in many churches who respond that way.

The antagonists soon realized that they would not be opposed by the silent majority. No one was going to stand up to them and rebuke their evil behavior. The passiveness of the majority who supported the minister actually encouraged these persons to step up the attack. I was reminded of the prime minister of England, Neville Chamberlain, who in 1938 signed the Munich Pact with the Axis powers. This policy of appeasement with Hitler actually encouraged Hitler to step up his aggression and begin World War II. Chamberlain did not have the stomach to challenge Hitler, and we know the rest of the story. Aggression always seeks to run over perceived weakness. I have seen this happen in a church as well.

Repeated Abuse

It was not until I announced early retirement that anything constructive was done about the antagonists in the church I served. Finally, the Sunday evening I resigned, the chairman of deacons mustered the courage to stand up and make the following statement: "Folks, our problem is not the pastor. Our problem is with the deacons. What I am about to say comes not from the chairman of deacons or from me as a deacon, but from me as just another member of the church. I move that all seventeen deacons be asked to resign and that a special committee be appointed to study and bring back a report regarding a new procedure for electing deacons, preferably a rotation plan."

The motion was passed by an overwhelming majority of the congregation. The antagonists sat stunned, stripped of their power, and helpless to do anything about it. They were indeed one angry bunch.

In a short time, most of this group of antagonists either left the church or moved out of town. The congregation needed a new minister, untainted by their history, so I resigned by taking early retirement and moved out of town myself. The church needed a fresh start under new leadership. Even though it took two full years to find a new minister, the interim period allowed for some healing to take place under the leadership of an outside interim pastor. Yet none of this horrible ordeal needed to have happened. Satan had had a heyday with this church. I only hope that by now they have learned how to keep this sort of damage from happening again.

If they have not learned their lesson, they will more than likely repeat this ordeal again and again. *Leadership*'s 1996 survey of terminated ministers showed that there are repeat-offender churches. This survey showed that 62 percent of forced-out ministers said that the church that terminated them had done it to one or more of their predecessors. Of those ministers who indicated their church had terminated others, 41 percent said the church had done it more than twice. Therefore, the survey concluded that churches that fire or force out their ministers will likely do it again.[9]

This was true of the church from which I retired under pressure. In the thirty years of their history, they had had eight pastors, none of whom had had a pleasant exit. I pray that the cycle of evil has stopped for them. But I wonder. A few of the antagonists are still there, probably just waiting for a leader to organize them and provide them a new rationale for their meanness. Evil seems never to die. It may lurk for a time in the shadows of piety, but if not restrained, it will arise to abuse again.

This problem is well analyzed by theologian David Wells who indicts the church for losing its moral vision, a keen sense of right and wrong based on the nature of God revealed in the Bible. He then concludes:

> This loss of moral categories, the loss of a transcendent sense of Good and Evil, does not, however, rid the world of those who are evil; it simply blinds us to the real nature of their actions. For now, evil becomes ordinary, routine, a part of life as natural and inevitable as cats killing mice.[10]

Is it possible that pathological antagonists and clergy abusers have become ordinary, routine, and a natural and inevitable part of the life of many churches? God help us if this is true.

4 The Minister's Greatest Enemy: Passive Lay Leaders

You would think, from all I have written thus far, that the minister's greatest enemy would be the clergy killers or the pathological antagonists. Not so. Recently I came across a quote by the ancient Roman philosopher Cicero: "There are two kinds of injustice: the first is found in those who do an injury, the second in those who fail to protect another from injury when they can."[1]

Cicero apparently considered these two kinds of injustice on the same level. I do not consider them so. The second is, in my judgment, much worse than the first. The first is due to either meanness or psychopathy. The second is due to either cowardice or indifference. I identify those who do an injury with the clergy killers and pathological antagonists. Passive lay leaders are those who fail to protect their minister from injury when they can. They observe the harm caused by the culprits but do nothing about it.

Most readers will recall the oft-quoted words of Edmund Burke, eighteenth-century British political philosopher: "All that is necessary for evil to triumph is for good men to do nothing." I have experienced this in a church where evil persons prevailed primarily because good but passive lay leaders chose to do nothing about them. The predominant viewpoint of the wounded ministers I have interviewed or corresponded with thus far agrees with me. It was bad enough being viciously attacked by caustic critics, but the greatest disappointment was the passiveness of those the wounded minister thought were his friends and supporters. They could have defended him but chose not to do so, either because they were afraid or because they didn't care.

Who can forget the scene in Shakespeare's immortal drama *Julius Caesar* where Caesar is being murdered by his antagonists, and he turns to see his friend Brutus stab him next? *Et tu Brute!*[2] ("And even you, Brutus!") His last thought was, *How could you, my friend, do this to me?* Ministers who have felt the blows of antagonists know how this feels.

Why Some Lay Leaders Cop Out

As a rule, ministers need a cadre of lay leadership to endorse, support, and encourage their ministry. They need men and women who are respected in the congregation to be advocates of their programs, ideas, and leadership in general. I have always had such a group in each of my pastoral posts. Without them, my hands would have been tied.

The minister's supporters are those godly people who drop by the church office from time to time to offer words of encouragement and to pray with the pastor, asking God to bless his efforts. These visits are like shots of spiritual adrenaline to the minister. They make his day! These supporters emulate the role of the biblical Barnabas, "son of encouragement." They are cheerleaders.

So why is it that when a minister is under attack by an antagonist or a small group of "uglies," some of those who are usually friends and supporters become thunderously silent, meek, and mild, and passively allow the attacks to continue unabated? I longed for the day when representative leaders of the silent majority would rise up and say to my antagonists, "Enough is enough. Stop this nonsense or leave the church. If you don't stop it or leave of your own accord, we will expel you ourselves. You have no right to batter our minister and drive him away." But those words never came. No advocate stood up to the critics to challenge their criticisms, even though most of them knew that the criticisms were full of outright false accusations and half-truth innuendoes. In the face of evil, silent friends are no friends at all.

Avoiding Conflict

Several possible dynamics are at work in the passiveness of supporters. Some laypersons have had their share of intrachurch conflict in the past when they lost friends over some conflictive issue. They don't want that to happen again. Their attitude may be expressed in the words, "The minister will eventually move on to another church, but the rest of us have to stay here and get along somehow." One deacon once told me that he had been involved in the conflict when the former pastor left, and he would never get involved again. So when I came under attack, this man and his wife, who had been so supportive and encouraging to me up until then, quickly withdrew into silence and absence. When we had key deacons' meetings where I needed his verbal support, he somehow had to work late that evening and could not attend. In the business meeting where my future was being discussed, this deacon and his wife chose to abstain from voting one way or the other. Having been burned once before, they had decided never to be burned again. They abandoned their pastor to the "wolves." I felt betrayed by their silence.

Intimidated by "Facts"

Others are simply intimidated by the more powerful and persuasive antagonists. Yes, they are afraid of them. Afraid of what? It is usually difficult to know. There is obviously no physical danger. Possible repercussions are more subtle. They may be afraid of being made to look foolish or ignorant in the face of the "facts" of the accusations. They could be thinking, *These critics may have information I don't possess; since I'm not really sure what or who to believe, I'll just wait this out and see what happens.* In the meantime, the minister's support dwindles. The antagonists see this and become even more bloodthirsty.

Some people are more easily intimidated than others. Antagonists are sometimes very persuasive and "charming" people. They always have the "truth" or the "facts" on their side, they contend.

I have known them to come into the church offices and meticulously pore over church records, bulletins, and files to accumulate
information that will support their contentions. When they attend
official church meetings to make their accusations, they bring with
them several pages of notes, files, and records to "substantiate"
their points. Such apparent documentation can easily intimidate
the unsuspecting leaders who want to support their minister.

I was once accused of excessive absence from the pulpit during
the previous year. It was church policy that I could be away up to
six Sundays per year for speaking engagements, conferences, or
other professional meetings. The two leading antagonists had read
through the church bulletins in the church office files for the fifty-
two Sundays of the previous year, and for each Sunday I was not
listed as preaching, they marked me down as being absent. They
counted ten such absences, four over the limit. They brought this
accusation before the next deacons' meeting. I was caught off guard
since I was not alerted to this charge in advance. I knew that I had
been absent only the allotted six Sundays, but I couldn't prove it
then, since I did not have the bulletin file for the year with me in
the meeting.

The next day I went into the office files and noted that four of
those "absences" were Sundays I was actually present but guest
speakers were listed as preachers of the day—two guest mission-
aries, a lay-witness speaker who had come to prepare the church
for an upcoming retreat, and a denominational executive invited
to promote a missions giving program. But the antagonists counted
those four Sundays as times the pastor was absent without leave.
At the next month's deacons' meeting, I brought this information
before these men, but to no avail. The antagonists, faced with the
true facts, simply changed the subject to another accusation. The
"silent faithful" said nothing. No one called for the antagonists to
admit their error and apologize. I was reminded of the Ku Klux
Klan's strategy of "smear and fear."

One antagonist once accused me before about fifteen people
meeting in a home of using the church phone to make personal
long-distance calls at church expense. I was flabbergasted. I knew
that I had done no such thing. From his "notes" he said I had
called a number in Dade County, Florida, to speak to a friend. All
I could say at the moment was I didn't do it. I returned to the

church office and pulled up the phone bills. I found one call to Miami, Florida, during the previous month, but it was on the church day-school phone bill, not the church office phone bill. I called the day-school director and asked her if she had made such a call. She readily admitted it, saying she had called one of her school suppliers to place an order, something she did almost every month. When I confronted my accuser with the facts, he gave me his usual smirky grin and tried to change the subject. I wrote a letter to those fifteen people to explain what really happened, but no one said anything, no apologies, no response whatever from anyone. The damage had been done. This reminds me of the typical hit-and-run driver who never pays for his crime. Unlike the driver, however, an antagonist enjoys doing this sort of thing.

The Force of Personality

Not only does the "appearance of facts" intimidate some people, the sheer force of antagonists' personalities unnerves passive people who are shy and nonconfrontive. Jack and Jim were both verbally persuasive, slick, and charming in presenting their arguments against the pastor, whether in meetings of certain groups or privately on the telephone to selected individuals.

A denominational executive once came to our church to observe some of our meetings. He later commented to me: "These fellows (the antagonists) are really powerful people, aren't they? Their personalities seem to overwhelm the others, intimidate them, leave them speechless. It is obvious to me that they are intensely angry about something deeply rooted in their past, but regardless of what is motivating them, they will probably succeed in running you off. No one is resisting them. The silent majority are leaving you standing alone. I don't see how you are able to stand up under the pressure as well as you are."

Too Busy

Another reason some lay leaders cop out in protecting the minister from pathological antagonists is their own extreme busyness in the jobs where they must earn a living. This coupled with the excessive free time of the antagonists creates an environment in which the antagonists have opportunity to operate. My supporters tended to be very busy people, putting in a heavy forty-hour (or more) workweek, along with their regular family duties. They simply haven't had much extra time to get embroiled in church politics. The antagonists have tended to be retired people (in one situation they were all retired military people in their fifties and early sixties) with a lot of free time on their hands.

There were critical times when attacks would come and I would try to contact my supporters for advice only to find them either out of town on business or unavailable at work. They did not have time to "prepare a defense" for me when the attacks came at official board meetings or church business meetings. The antagonists had plenty of time to plan their strategy, organize their supporters, hold secret planning meetings with their friends, and spend numerous hours telephoning people to get out the vote for key meetings. My supporters were like a National Guard unit being called up to fight a full-time, seasoned, and well-armed military unit.

The Loneliness of a Minister under Attack

When clergy are being abused by church bullies, and key lay leaders do little or nothing to stop it, the minister is usually all alone and feels it deeply. Those who should be rushing to his defense are seemingly nonexistent or strangely and disappointingly silent. There were many days when I sincerely wondered if God really cared about what was happening. During many weekdays, I would go into our large empty auditorium to pray. I prayed intensely and earnestly. My prayers seemed to go nowhere. I felt as if God had "gone fishing." No one came to encourage me. I have never felt so alone in all my life. I knew exactly how Elijah felt: "I alone am left, and they are seeking my life, to take it away" (1 Kings 19:10). I now realize looking retrospectively that God was not really absent and, as with Elijah, he was working, protecting, and providing all along. But at the time, I felt very much alone and abandoned.

Loneliness is one of the worst of all psychological wounds. We humans are social creatures in every possible way. Isolation is one of the worst of punishments because of our socially dependent nature.

Wounded ministers easily identify with Samuel Taylor Coleridge's lines from *The Rime of the Ancient Mariner:*

> Alone, alone, all, all alone;
> Alone on a wide, wide sea.
> And never a saint took pity on
> My soul in agony.
> . . . .
> Like one that on a lonesome road
> Doth walk in fear and dread,
> And having once turned round, walks on,
> And turns no more his head;
> Because he knows a frightful fiend
> Doth close behind him tread.
> . . . .
> This soul hath been
> Alone on a wide, wide sea;
> So lonely 'twas, that God himself
> Scarce seemed there to be.[3]

No wonder that one of the worst punishments in prison is solitary confinement, total isolation from other humans. Our national space agency decided years ago never to send anyone into space alone for any extended period of time. Sustained loneliness has been known to drive humans insane. Even children's workers in day schools know that isolating a misbehaving child can be a very effective form of discipline. But the child interprets it as psychological punishment if it lasts very long.

It is no different for ministers who feel cut off from the psychological support of their key lay leaders. Ministers who feel this kind of loneliness are not weak; they are simply normal human beings who are socially conditioned to expect support from those who once pledged to follow their leadership. This kind of loneliness is indeed a very real wound, an injury that requires healing just as much as a physical wound does.

Standing alone against pathological antagonists without strong support and defense from supposedly godly lay leaders makes the minister feel betrayed. It is the feeling of an army officer in the heat of battle leading his troops against the enemy only to discover that his men have run in retreat and left him to stand alone.

If you are one of these passive lay leaders who has failed to stand up against those who have unjustly and cruelly sought to get rid of a minister in your church, you need to take stock of your actions. God expects you to stand by and with his leader. Just as Moses needed Aaron and Hur to hold up his hands during the battle with Amalek at Rephidim (Exod. 17:8–16), so your minister needs you to hold him up and support him during the spiritual battles the church wages. Unfortunately some of the church's most heated battles are fought within the congregation where people with the Diotrephes complex set about to wreak havoc by attacking the church's ordained clergy leaders. If these church bullies are allowed to get away with such mayhem, the church will suffer immeasurably. How can you passively and sheepishly stand aside, look the other way, and allow this to happen?

To paraphrase the Golden Rule, "Do for others what you would have them do for you." Ministers under attack need protectors to come to their defense. Put yourself in the shoes of an abused clergyperson. What would you expect from those who once pledged support for your ministry? A vote to call a minister to a church position is also a pledge to support that person in every possible way.

Do not allow your fear and feelings of intimidation to place you in the camp of the minister's greatest enemy. Place yourself in the position of Aaron and Hur who saw Moses, even though a great and powerful leader, still in need of support and upholding. Without those two brave men, Israel would have lost the battle. Their role was simple—uphold the leadership of Moses. Yes, even Moses was in need of support and encouragement. Your minister is no different.

Passivity Enables Meanness

Passive lay leaders must eventually bear the responsibility for *enabling* the misbehavior of pathological antagonists and clergy killers. Call this the Neville Chamberlain complex. To repeat, the minister's greatest enemies are not the pathological antagonists or the clergy killers but the cowardly, silent lay leaders who refuse to protect their minister from abuse by mustering the courage to do so.

Silent supporters are no supporters. A wounded minister needs a cadre of vocal supporters who will rise up and face the abusers with a loud, "Stop this ungodly abuse, and stop it now, or we will eject you from this congregation." Then action should follow their words.

What can the good and godly lay persons in a church do to support their ministers and restrain clergy abusers? I will give specific details later in this book, particularly in chapters 5 and 11 on how lay leaders can be their minister's "bodyguards and cheerleaders."

In the meantime, I want to share the following true story that illustrates in a humorous yet powerful way what lay leaders can do to protect their ministers. A friend of mine had just been called to be the pastor of a large metropolitan church in the west. He was to succeed a pastor who had served that church for more than twenty-five years and chose to retire early. Three of the church's younger deacons met one morning for coffee.

All three were distressed over the way their pastor had resigned. One spoke up and said, "You fellows know what a wonderful pastor we had, but he chose to retire early because of one of our elderly deacons who gave our pastor trouble over the past several years. His criticisms were unwarranted and unjust. We've got to stop this from ever happening again." The other two agreed wholeheartedly.

They devised the following plan. They called the pastor's antagonist and invited him to go with them to see a special place. Not knowing what the plan was, he agreed. The three young deacons drove by and picked the elderly deacon up at his house and then drove out north of the city to the banks of a river.

They invited the older deacon to step out of the car, telling him they wanted to show him something special, which turned out to be a large cottonwood tree. The spokesman of the three then said, "We want you to remember this tree. We all know that our beloved pastor resigned in tears over the way you treated him for the past several years, and we have decided that the rest of us should not have allowed that to happen. We are here to repent of our silence over what you did. We have just called a new pastor who will be here in three weeks, and we have made a vow here under this tree that we will not allow you to antagonize him, so don't even think about causing any trouble. This is why this tree is a special place for all of us."

My friend then concluded, "You know, I served that church for several years and never had one ounce of trouble out of that older deacon. My predecessor, who remained in the church, never understood why. Well, it was obvious to me years later when those younger deacons told me the 'tree story' that they had decided to become my 'ministerial bodyguards.' Wouldn't it be nice if every church had some deacons like that!"

5 The Dangers of Autonomous Church Polity

It may seem strange, if not heretical, for a longtime Baptist to write a chapter dealing with the dangers of autonomous church polity. For years Baptists and other Free Church tradition churches have prided themselves on local church autonomy as the best and most biblical form of church government. This polity or form of government places ultimate authority in the hands of the local congregation rather than a hierarchy outside the local church or a ruling board of elders, deacons, or some other small group empowered by the church.

In the New Testament, local church autonomy seems to be the prevailing method of government, although in some instances there was apostolic authority where one or more of the apostles made key decisions. In other instances, a plurality of elders was looked to for leadership decisions. Deacons, however, were clearly identified as servant ministers of the congregation to do the congregation's bidding. That's why they were set apart in the first place. The word *deacon* comes from the Greek word *diakonos,* which means servant. It can also be translated minister, but what is a minister but a servant of a higher authority!

So what does local autonomous church polity have to do with abused and wounded ministers, whether pastors or other church staff ministers? Let me explain.

A Sociological Reality

Any social organization must have leadership, which implies that the majority of the group is made up of followers. But in a local congregation, which supposedly rules itself, the leadership is generally elected by the congregation and charged with leadership responsibilities. These leaders are allegedly accountable back to the congregation.

Unfortunately the ideal local church autonomous form of government does not work that way. There is a sociological reality at work: Any self-governing body of people ends up being governed by a small group; an oligarchy we call it (the rule of the few). Two forms of oligarchy can be observed in any local church. The first is some type of official board (deacons, elders), elected by the church in accordance with its constitution and bylaws and is what sociologists call the manifest or official governing group. The second is what sociologists call the latent or unofficial group of self-appointed leaders who are not necessarily elected by the church.

The official or publicly recognized leader of a church is usually the pastor/minister, an ordained clergyperson, who preaches and does pastoral care and day-to-day church administration. In many if not most churches, however, there is an unofficial lay leader who may not even have an elected position, but most people in the church know who he is and that he rules the congregation from behind the scenes. Any new pastor who goes to lead such a church had better find out as soon as possible who that person is and try to get along with him and be his friend if he can.

This unofficial lay leader may be a kind of "elder statesman" among a group of similar lay leaders. Such a group is normally not very large—five or six people on average, occasionally as many as ten in a large church. But one is the unofficial head. Nothing really important is decided without his prior approval. Any new programs to be recommended by the pastor need to be cleared in private by this unofficial leader. To try to run a program without his approval will probably bring the kiss of death on the idea. For the pastor or any church staff person to go straight to the congregation with an idea or program will usually prove to be a foolish action. It won't succeed if there is an unofficial lay leader, with longevity of authority in the eyes of the congregation, who is ignored or bypassed.

In a church with an entrenched oligarchy, a minister who tries to lead without their approval will be a short-term minister. A power struggle will develop because a lay oligarchy will consider its authority being challenged by such a "reckless" minister who "doesn't know his place" in the church. As one such powerful lay leader said to me, "We hire and fire the pastor; we pay him to do what we tell him; the nerve of him to ignore us!" In such churches, sad as it sounds, the minister is little more than a glorified custodian, a chaplain of sorts to them, a hireling of a small group of movers and shakers in the congregation.

Certainly a wise minister will try to work with the elected lay leaders in the congregation, whatever they are called. He should take into his confidence his lay leaders whether they are serving on elected committees or the official board. But some churches have become stagnated with a small group of power-hungry persons who are more concerned with holding onto their power positions, whether official or unofficial, than with what is best for the church. Actually the thought of a vibrant and growing church is considered a threat by those holding long-term power positions. A growing number of new members, especially young, vibrant, and intelligent adults, can pose a real threat to older lay leaders who enjoy their entrenched power positions. A minister who can attract and enlist such new members will find that these new members are more loyal to him than to the older established leaders. This may threaten the oligarchy. When so threatened, they will often lead an effort to get rid of this popular minister who is "shaking things up," which they interpret as eroding their power base.

The unfortunate thing about a church that has grown from a small size to a larger congregation over the years is that local church autonomy becomes unwieldy and impractical. Probably a congregation of more than three hundred will discover this reality. Since in most instances in contemporary society ministers tend to come and go rather frequently, leadership defaults into the hands of long-term recognized lay leaders. A new minister cannot immediately earn the respected role of the leader of the congregation, at least not in any practical sense. It takes at least five years to earn such respect and trust. Lay leaders who enjoy a powerful leadership role, whether elected or not, do not easily give up or share this power. Therefore a conflict of leadership may result.

Every new pastor must ask this question on arrival to assume the pastoral leadership role to which the church has called him: *In reality who is running this church?* Most pastor search committees are oblivious to the true answer, do not want to discuss this reality, or actually deceive the prospective minister with such platitudes as, "We are a democratically governed congregation that rules itself."

Sometimes pastor search committees are extremely naive about the oligarchy that runs their church. In my last pastorate I learned within a few months after arrival that none of the ruling small group was represented on the committee that brought me there. I could look back and see that when I met with the finance committee to discuss my salary package, the chairman of that committee was the "unofficial head of the church" who believed that if he could control the financial decisions of the church, then he could control the church. He was able to persuade the pastor search committee to set my salary package at several thousand dollars less than I was earning in my then current position with the promise that when the next budget went into effect (four months later), my salary would match what I had been making. I foolishly agreed without any attempt on my part to negotiate a parallel move. That decision cost me about two thousand dollars that year plus some benefits that had been part of my previous position's remuneration package.

While we trust God to take care of us financially, we still must be wise as serpents if we are in a position of negotiating our salary. Otherwise in the long run the ruthless misers of the church will not generally respect us and will take advantage of us in other ways. The above mentioned pastor search committee was easily intimidated by the finance committee chairman and his supporters with whom he had personally stacked his committee. As it turned out, this chairman was an antagonist who functioned as the unofficial head of the church. He didn't want to serve on the pastor search committee because it would be too much work for a man his age who was in poor health, but he was determined to control any pastor they would recommend.

This same man once commented to our very fine deacon chairman, "I don't believe you should ever get close to a pastor. You can't trust those fellows. They don't earn the money we pay them." I came to discover that the reason he felt this way was that he had developed the habit of challenging the leadership of every pastor he had ever had, which resulted in a power struggle and the eventual termination of the pastor. Consequently he knew it would be emotionally difficult to run off a pastor he had gotten close to. It's hard to fire a friend.

There must be an answer to this sociological reality. Is there a realistic and practical way to deal with it? I have some suggestions.

Democratic Leadership and Pastoral Authority

The prevailing pattern of government among the churches in the New Testament appears to be a democratic one, where the local congregation made most of the major decisions. The record of the church's decision to recognize God's inclusion of the Gentiles into the church (in Acts 15) is a clear example of this type of decision making. However, apostolic and pastoral authority being recognized by the congregation of believers is also to be observed. This was not a heavy-handed dictatorship by one or a few of these recognized leaders. They were gentle shepherds leading the people to sense the presence of the risen Christ in their midst as well as a sensitivity to the will of their Lord in these congregational matters.

The authority of the apostles and pastors was one of an earned respect for their position in the church. It involved a conviction on the part of the congregation that the authority of these leaders had been delegated by the Head of the church, Jesus Christ. There were no arrogant, power-hungry challengers to this authority in the churches discussed by Luke in Acts. The first challenge to such authority does not develop until Paul confronts certain Judaizers in 2 Corinthians (chapters 10–13 reveal his response to them) and later when John rebukes one Diotrephes, who challenged both John and the church (see 3 John).

The early Christians generally recognized pastoral authority as delegated leadership from the Lord and believed that he would hold these pastors accountable for any failure to lead the church aright. For deacons or some official board of laymen to treat their pastor or other ministers on staff as second-class hirelings is totally foreign to the New Testament. God expects a church's lay leadership to respect and follow the leadership of their pastor; otherwise how can he be considered a leader? Why have a pastor if you are not going to follow him as the shepherd (the meaning of *pastor*) of the congregation? Why not just hire a Sunday preacher?

I once heard the pastor of a very large church in Houston, Texas, say that a deacon-led church will not be a growing church. That has been my observation and experience also. My last pastorate is in an excellent location in a major metropolitan area. Its auditorium will seat 1,100, but attendance has ranged from 200 to 400 in recent years. It is currently averaging about 250. For more than thirty years it has, for the most part, been led by a small group of deacon lay leaders. If the eight pastors of the church during this time had been vigorously and enthusiastically followed, the attendance could easily have reached the 1,000 range. But the lay oligarchy has consistently challenged and resisted the pastor's leadership, resulting in an impasse of leadership that caused an unpleasant exit by each of the eight pastors. Consequently this church has a terrible reputation in the community as being a "fussy" church. Many new members soon leave the church and go elsewhere because, as one young father told me, "Pastor, we love and respect your leadership, but my wife and I will not expose our children to the conflict that is so obvious in this church." I saw several young families leave for the same reason. When these families left the church, the oligarchy blamed the pastor for the decline in attendance.

During a business meeting in this church, the personnel committee brought a recommendation that a volunteer staff person be recognized as an assistant to the pastor. This man was an ordained minister who worked in a secular job but who desired a place of ministry assisting the pastor in any capacity needed in his spare time. There would be no salary considerations; he just wanted a place to serve as a volunteer assistant to the pastor. I had followed the official policies and procedures of the church bylaws for recommending such a staff position. But the oligarchy decided that since I had not first gotten their approval, they would exert their power and oppose the recommendation of the committee. They saw it as the pastor's idea, not theirs. Consequently one antagonist made a stirring speech to the church that this was a terrible idea reflecting "poor leadership" on the part of the pastor, but no evidence was cited for such a conclusion. It was a nasty scene in the congregational meeting. Suspicions were raised. Fears were exploited.

In attendance that evening was a relatively new family in our church, a man and his wife with their five children. This man stood up after a lot of debate over the motion and said, "We have been members here for about three months. The pastor is a godly man who preaches the Bible. His vision for the church appeals to us, but the conflict in this church is appalling. We came from a church in another state that was vibrant and growing. There we followed the pastor's leadership. If he said to paint the church yellow, we painted it yellow! He was God's man to lead our church, and we followed him. It paid off, to say the least. But some of you people in this church think you are the leader. No wonder you are not growing. If this negative atmosphere doesn't change, my family and I will be looking for another church." And they did. Within a month they were gone, because the conflict didn't stop.

I am not recommending a blind following of a pastor. Some churches are afflicted with pastoral leadership that never considers any differing views. The answer is certainly not pastoral dictatorship. Some pastors are so insecure that they have to control everything that happens in the church. This usually results in ministerial burnout. No pastor wears an S on his undershirt; he is not Superman.

A Ministers' Advisory Council

I recommend a ministers' advisory council, made up of both men and women, young and old, a cross section of the congregation if at all possible. (The details of organizing this council will be discussed in chapter 11.) The pastor should have a major voice in the selection of the council members but so should the official board and the congregation. This council should serve as advisors to the ministerial staff on a regular basis, at least four times a year, but more often if needed.

Such a council would be in a position, by church authority, to deal with any pathological antagonists or clergy killers who emerge in the life of the congregation. This would serve to keep troublemakers in check. Antagonists are more likely to behave themselves if they recognize that they could be brought before such a council to account for their actions, even though such initial accountability would be confidential.

It is common practice for some university and seminary presidents to have an advisory council, separate from the official board of trustees. This council functions as a sounding board for the president's ideas and also as idea people to make suggestions the president may not have thought about. This could work in a local church as well.

A problem in setting this council in place might be the official board's possible perception of it being a threat to their leadership role. But this fear could be defused by adequate explanation as to the council's role and function.

The traditional autonomous church polity allows the antagonist to misbehave behind the scenes and get away with it. To say that the official board is accountable to the congregation does not usually work very well, practically speaking. They need to be accountable to a smaller group of supporters and advisors of the pastor and his staff. This is not a foolproof idea, but it is far better than no such group of advisors. In the final analysis, any group's quality of performance is dependent on the quality and spirit of the persons who comprise the group.

Some churches, United Methodists for example, have what they call a Pastor–Parish Relations Committee, separate from the official board or the administrative council. However, it helps if the congregation empowers such an advisory group with the authority to bring recommendations before the congregation. Yes, it could include recommending disciplinary action of a wayward and stubborn minister. Occasionally, there are such. But they could also recommend disciplinary action of a pathological antagonist in the congregation or on the official board.

Another important point to make with regard to the makeup of a ministers' advisory council is the significant role women can have in such a group. Since most official boards are composed of men, they sometimes have a tendency to allow an antagonistic male to do harm to a minister. It has been my observation through many years of service in churches that when women serve in key leadership positions, men tend to behave themselves better when it comes to power struggles. Even though a growing number of churches elected women to positions of lay leadership in the last years of the twentieth century, a majority of churches still reserves lay leadership roles for males. Even in the New Testament, we find at least one clearly identified woman deacon by the name of Phoebe who is called "a deacon [Gk. *diakonos*] of the church at Cenchreae" (Rom. 16:1). The well-known Greek New Testament scholar at the Southern Baptist Theological Seminary in Louisville, Kentucky, for many years, the late A. T. Robertson, unquestionably recognized Phoebe as a female deacon.[1] Much recent conservative New Testament scholarship reveals a growing conviction that the leadership role of women in the early church was much more significant than most of the churches today have been willing to admit.

It is my conviction that the male pathological antagonists I have had to deal with in the local church would have behaved more civilly had their wives or other women been present in official board meetings. I well remember one evening, after the conclusion of a nasty church business meeting, when one antagonist verbally attacked me at the front of the church. His wife took him by the arm, saying, "I'm taking you home. You're in no mood to talk to anyone." Then she led him up the aisle toward the door. She was not a domineering woman, but she knew how to control her angry husband. This is one reason why some domineering males do not want women to be elected as deacons or official board members. Women know how to cramp their style of control!

Autonomous church polity is, in my judgment, biblical, and it best affords the opportunity for lay members to develop into leaders, but it has its dangers also. I trust my recommendations can help to mitigate those dangers and allow the local church to respect and follow the leadership of the shepherd of the congregation along with his minister associates.

Chapter eleven will present a fuller description of a ministers' advisory council.

6 Wrecking a Minister's Life and Career

When pathological antagonists and clergy killers attack a minister maliciously and persistently, the minister's life and career will be gravely affected. Such animosity will gradually and possibly inevitably wreck that minister's life and career in a number of ways. I have been gathering numerous testimonies or stories from a large number of ministers who have been unjustly terminated from their church positions as a result of these attacks. After rereading a number of them in preparation for writing this chapter, I was overcome by a deep sense of sadness. This cumulative reading of these cases of abused clergy left me almost in clinical depression because I could readily identify with most of them from my own experience.

These stories were given to me with the hope that I would share them with the readers of this book, guaranteeing, of course, anonymity. Some of the details have been slightly altered to protect the identities of the persons involved. All names have been changed as well. But the basic content of the stories remains true to the experience.

Shattered Hopes and Dreams

Some general observations from the accounts shared with me are in order. First, many of these individuals were abused in their early adult years of ministry in their first or second church assignments. They were fresh out of college and/or seminary full of excitement, hope, and vision regarding their call to ministry. Call them visionaries or idealists if you wish, but their heart was in the right place. They were committed to preach the gospel and build strong churches; they were determined to do the will of God in and through their lives; they had dedicated their abilities, talents, and spiritual gifts to extending the kingdom of God wherever God sent them.

Many of them were extremely naive as to the sociological and psychological nature of the church. They had never seen secular power politics played out in a local church. They were generally uninformed about the presence of pathological antagonists and clergy killers among the people of God. It was difficult for them to accept the reality that such persons often operate in the power structure of a local church. They were shocked when first attacked but even more shocked when "the good people" they had learned to trust and respect failed to come to the defense of their minister who was being abused. They were puzzled to find so-called Christians acting in such an unchristian manner.

When the abuse and lack of defense became intolerable, the hopes and dreams of these idealistic ministers were shattered almost beyond repair. Their first and most traumatic struggle was with the inevitable questions, Where is God? Why would God allow such things to happen in his own church? If this kind of conflict is allowed to happen in a congregation of God's people and the non-Christians are turned off by it (the very people we are trying to reach), doesn't God care? The Scriptures warn believers of possible persecution, but from within the church itself? The hopes and dreams of winning a vast number of people to Jesus Christ were crushed. Fractured hopes and dreams are extremely difficult to restore.

As a result of shattered expectations and deep vocational wounds inflicted in or by a church, a wounded minister can become quite bitter if not cynical about a calling to ministry. Most of the persons who shared their experiences of abuse in a church reflected deep bitterness, and bitter ministers can easily end up with wrecked lives and careers. I have known several servants of God who have been persecuted by non-Christian outsiders, such as political or business figures in a community or nation, especially on a foreign mission field. None of them became bitter about their call to ministry. Yet when ministers are abused by so-called people of God, who hold powerful leadership positions in a church, that has been another story. Christian servants expect, and rightly so, to be supported and encouraged by fellow believers in the church. When a church attacks its own ministers, those wounded servants rarely recover. Spiritual bitterness is extremely toxic to one's faith.[1]

Most of the abused clergy I have interviewed are now engaged in some kind of secular work outside of a church position. Most of them still belong to and attend a local church but avoid any leadership role that might expose them to abuse again. They have never recovered their original hopes and dreams for ministry. No longer will they trust established lay leaders in a congregation. As one said, "If you ever get burned in a church, you will intentionally stay away from the fire, and especially so if members of your family also got charred."

Most of the wounded ministers I have counseled are college and/or seminary trained, well-equipped professionally by godly academic mentors. Yet many seminaries do not prepare their students to deal with antagonists. A book like this should be added to their training curriculum. Sitting on the sidelines of ministry, able to lead, teach, and preach in a productive way, they are too wounded to minister in a pastoral role again, at least for now. What a waste! Thousands of dollars and hours of time spent in preparing to serve the church have been dissipated by vicious lay leaders (or senior pastors) who thought they were doing God a service by interfering with and/or terminating these ministers with whom they disagreed.

Almost none of these stories shared with me involved the church seeking outside professional expertise in resolving the conflict that resulted in the expulsion of the minister. Such help is often available. Most church denominational offices, on either state or national levels, either have or can refer a church to such experts.[2] However, such expertise is rarely sought. This is to be expected when the antagonists are in charge. They don't want any outsiders interfering with their power. They reason that it is less expensive simply to get rid of the minister and get another one. The facts of experience show that this is false economizing, but the real crux of the issue is that this strategy of running the minister off is against the spirit of Christ. He would never do this. Besides, spending some money to resolve conflict in a church in the long run will pay rich dividends both financially and spiritually. Moreover, how can we measure the life and career of a minister of the gospel in dollars and cents?

First Dysfunctional Church

Pastor Bob, fresh out of seminary, lasted less than one year at his first church. Here is his story:

"Looking back, I should have realized it was a death trap for pastors." Only two pastors in the church's one hundred-plus-year history had ever served more than two years. One of the deacons told me they were the only two who had not been fired. My predecessor served four and one-half years, the longest tenure in church history. Recently, I found out that my successor also lasted less than two years before he too was fired.

"The church had three elderly men who were 'life deacons.' They ruled everything. They had some insane rules that they placed on me as pastor: (1) Part of my job description was to mow the church grass, change the light bulbs, type and fold the bulletin, and lock and unlock the church; (2) I had to spend part of every day at the church so they could see my car and make sure I was working; (3) I was not to go 'far away' on my day off, and if I wanted to go out of town overnight I had to get permission (and I could only be away one night!). One deacon actually told me he watched for my car to see when I got back to town at night. I know this sounds surreal, but while there, I got to know my predecessor, and he told me they abused him in the same way.

"In addition to the deacons, there was one couple who abused me. They were not members and refused to join (!), but since they gave considerable sums of money to the church, they had attained the status of members. One evening in their home they told me that my job was to do 'whatever they told me to do.' They said they could tell me this because 'You are like the last pastor, a snotty-nosed kid who doesn't know anything.' They arrived at Sunday school one-half hour before anyone else and expected me to be there to entertain them. Generally their abuse was more covert; other pastors in the community told me they talked negatively about me behind my back. For instance, I found out from our deacon chairman that they offered to pay the entire church's budget the next year if they could select the church's pastor, because they did not like me. The deacons, especially the chairman, criticized me on several occasions for not treating this couple with enough respect.

"My worst experience of abuse came from an elderly woman named Vivian who was so crazy that I still wonder if she might have been demon-possessed. One night at our midweek service, she stopped me in the middle of my Bible study and asked me in a loud voice where I got my inspiration. 'Was it from books or from God?' She obviously did not like my answer, so she responded that there was nothing Spirit-filled about my preaching and teaching and that I should throw away my books. She continued on this tirade for more than five minutes, humiliating me in front of the congregation. I was shaken to the core. After church was over, only a few people spoke to me, and all they said was, 'Well, preacher, you aren't the first.' A few months later, during Sunday school opening assembly, she repeated her tirade against me. None of the deacons or other leaders sought to contain her or to speak in my support.

"This woman, Vivian, accused me of everything she could think of. All of her accusations were lies; there was not one grain of truth in any of them. She was also convinced that I was lazy. She would drive by the church several times a day and count how often my car was there and report her findings to the deacons. Another time she measured the church grass with a yardstick and decided it was too high to suit her, so she also reported that to the deacons.

"Vivian also tried to control my day off. On one occasion I announced to the church that I was going on my day off to the nearby seminary to do library research for sermons (since the deacons had earlier ordered me to announce to the church how I was using my day off). When Vivian heard about this, she asked the deacons to dock one day's pay from my salary. During a visit to her home, she told me, 'You are the cause of all the problems in our church, and you need to leave for the church to get itself straightened out.' When I mentioned her outbursts to the deacons, the chairman again criticized me for not treating her with enough respect.

"I got into trouble with the church for 'changing everything,' especially the music. The church treasurer actually spent one midweek service marking hymns in the hymnal and told me to place only those hymns he marked in the order of worship! Also, I was young with a seminary education, but I did not 'throw my coat on the floor and stomp on it when I preached.' They wanted me to be more emotional. Culturally the church and I could not have been farther apart.

"What ultimately got me fired was a premarital counseling incident. A young woman who had visited the church but was not a member came to me with her fiancé for premarital counseling. One of the topics I always discuss in premarital counseling is sex. In this case I merely gave them some Christian materials on sex and asked them to discuss them. Everything we discussed was supposed to be confidential. Without my knowledge or permission the young woman gave the materials to her mother, who gave them to the deacon chairman's wife, who gave them to her husband. At the next deacons' meeting the chairman exploded at me, saying sex was a personal matter and that I had no right to discuss it with anyone. I was never allowed to counsel this young couple again.

"A couple of days later, another pastor in our area came by my house to tell me that he had just talked with our deacon chairman who told him that he was going to make a motion at the next church business meeting to have me fired. I called the deacon chairman and asked for a private meeting with him. He then told me he had heard rumors in the church and community that 'I undressed women with my eyes.' I was never alone with any women. Moreover, he echoed Vivian's claim that the offerings and attendance were down, and it was my fault. He said that the premarital counseling incident was the last straw. He urged me to resign the following Sunday or else he would fire me. So I resigned. The day I left that church and town and returned to my hometown in another state was the happiest day of my life because I knew that the church there could no longer beat me up for things I never did."

For the next two years, the young minister was out of the ministry working in a secular job. He was too injured to take another church position or preach again. It took these two years for his wounds to heal. This church almost wrecked his life and ministry, but eventually God restored him. He is back in ministry today, but the scars remain.

Prince of Peace Fighting Church

Pastor Harold was the minister of the church for nearly six years, yet the real "boss" of the church was an arrogant, mean-spirited lawyer who was known as the Judge (because for a couple of years he had been the local municipal court judge). Judge Walsh was a very large man (weighing some three hundred pounds) with dark eyebrows and piercing eyes. He always wore a black suit and tie. During Pastor Harold's final year at this church, control issues came to a head. Mr. Walsh had been chairman of deacons for about twenty-five years straight, and the church had been in some kind of internal conflict for those twenty-five years. Most everyone saw the connection but no one was courageous enough to do anything about it.

Pastor Harold had been a professional boxer during his twenties. When he later entered the ministry, he brought his strong personality with him into the pulpit. He really was a wonderful, caring man. Although a "fighter," he used his fighting spirit against various social evils outside the church (for example, the alcohol industry). However, local beer distributors brought considerable business pressure against some of the businessmen who were deacons in Pastor Harold's church. Their message: Either get rid of your pastor or we will ruin your businesses.

In addition, Pastor Harold and Judge Walsh were usually locked in some kind of power struggle. Deacons' meetings often consisted of the judge leading the board in blocking the pastor's programs. Once a year, the deacons had the task of recommending any salary or benefits raises for the pastor to the church budget committee. Walsh made sure no raises were recommended. He could always marshal ten reasons against them. The majority of the deacons always meekly acquiesced to Walsh's wishes.

During Pastor Harold's sixth year, Walsh began circulating the idea that "our church is a four-year church." Consequently Pastor Harold was long overdue in leaving. Since Pastor Harold was the only pastor this church had ever had who dared to stand up to the judge, Walsh became quite militant in organizing a movement to terminate Pastor Harold's tenure.

Monthly business meetings were usually horrible: Walsh and his lackeys would make cutting comments on the church floor about Pastor Harold's leadership. Regardless of what the subject was under consideration, they accused the pastor of being "a poor leader." Yet the facts ran counter to all of their accusations: Attendance was higher than ever, new members joined every Sunday, the number of annual baptisms was up over past statistics, the budget was being met if not oversubscribed, parking was a problem, and so on.

The stress, however, began to get the best of both Pastor Harold and his wife. Health problems began to develop. Late-night harassing phone calls were made to the parsonage. Ugly anonymous letters were mailed regularly to the pastor and his wife. News of secret meetings of Walsh and the deacons at Walsh's house or office began to be made known. These meetings obviously had one item on their agenda: Bash the pastor. Since Pastor Harold was already in his mid-fifties, it would not be easy for him to find another church of comparable size that would be willing to call a man his age. But he knew that he and especially his wife could not last much longer.

Pastor Harold was very good at personal evangelism, so he spent most of his time that last year doing just that. The baptistry was used almost every Sunday. Of course, the conflict in the church puzzled these new Christians, and it deeply disturbed Pastor Harold that these new converts might become disillusioned over what the church was all about. Several people stopped attending because they, as several said, "did not want to raise their children in such a harsh and conflicted church environment."

The final week of Pastor Harold's ministry was one no minister would want to remember. Pastor Harold's wife was sick at home with a stress-related illness. That last Sunday morning, the pastor baptized several new converts. The worship service was full with more than six hundred present. Word was out that something was about to happen. Pastor Harold preached a powerful sermon on Jesus being taunted to "come down off the cross" and quit his mission to be the suffering Servant. He chose to directly address the problem by saying near the end of his sermon: "None of these troublemakers in our church has ever won a single person to

Christ." The wife of one of Walsh's lieutenants who had been an outspoken critic of the pastor stood up in the back of the auditorium and shouted, "Pastor Harold, that's not so!" The pastor responded, "Sit down, Mrs. Sowers, you're out of order." Many of the elderly women in the church shrieked in shock at such a public display.

The deacons announced a called business meeting for that Wednesday evening. Judge Walsh had rounded up every person he could to vote on the anticipated resignation of the pastor. Some were not even members of the church.

The pastor had sent his resignation by a friend who read it to the church. Many supportive comments were made on behalf of Pastor Harold, but many ugly things were said, especially by Judge Walsh. One very elderly gentleman commented to the associate pastor after the meeting, "When Judge Walsh was speaking against the pastor, I could see the devil in his eyes!"

Before the meeting was dismissed, about 250 people who loved the pastor got up and left in disgust. They had been outvoted regarding the pastor's resignation. The next Sunday this group met to start a new church. In time this new church became the leading evangelical church in town, much larger than Prince of Peace Fighting Church. The latter church has never recovered from this debacle, continuing to make the same mistakes for several years. It did help some when Judge Walsh finally died.

In a few weeks after his resignation, Pastor Harold and his wife moved to a major city in their state where he had been offered a national denominational consulting position in which he served until his retirement. He never served as a pastor again. His pastoral ministry had been wrecked. His life would never be the same again. Both he and his wife (as well as their adult children) had to deal with a lot of bitterness about the local church for several years.

First Church of No Compassion

Pastor Dave had been at his church for six years when things began to fall apart. A midsize congregation of about 200 in morning worship, most of the families had been part of the church for several generations. The church was over 150 years old at this time.

Dave's predecessor had been at the church for 23 years but left under pressure. Dave arrived to lead a divided and fairly well demoralized congregation. Here is his story:

"In 1991 I was involved in several things. I began a doctor of ministry program at a distant seminary. I was involved in several community activities, including serving as a volunteer chaplain at the local county hospital. The church was refurbishing facilities and beginning to plateau numerically. I spent much time in members' homes and places of business. Our third child was born that year. In June of 1991 my wife told me that she was dissatisfied with our marriage and she was ending all intimate contact (emotional as well as sexual). I sought counseling for myself from a pastoral counselor. In August my wife took the children and went to her parents' home in another state.

"I called together the church council to tell them what was happening. I thought I had kept it quiet, but several people later told me that they knew something was wrong but didn't know how to approach me. The council encouraged me to take three weeks off in order to sort out what I wanted to do and to give the congregation time to accept what had happened. Later that evening I met with the entire deacon council to share with them the news. Three of the younger deacons asked that I leave the room so they could talk freely. I later learned that they wanted a vote to dismiss me. Instead, the deacons voted eleven to ten to ask the church to approve the three weeks off. The congregation did so the following Sunday evening by a vote of 98 percent.

"After that meeting of the church, the deacon chairman asked me what I thought I would do. I told him I was going to be with my daughter for her first birthday, and I hoped to talk with my wife about our future. He asked me if I thought I would stay as pastor. I told him I did not know but that I thought it was unlikely. I said that I needed to put my energy into keeping my family together. The night before I left, the deacon chairman called to ask me to meet with him. When he came to my house, he told me that he and some of the other deacons had met and concluded that I wasn't planning on returning. Instead, they believed that I was simply trying to string them along, taking a salary and living in the parsonage while not really intending to return to the pulpit. They were going to call a deacons' meeting that week to demand that I be out of the parsonage by that weekend. I tried to reason with him, then argued with him, then finally told him that I would get an attorney. He left, telling me to be out of the parsonage and office by that weekend.

"I began calling those deacons whom I believed would support me, begging them to do something to stop the antagonists. Each of them said in effect, 'What they are doing to you is wrong, but I don't know what to do about it.' I called a church member who was a psychologist to ask him what to do, but he backed away from taking any initiative (it would hurt his practice). After calling several others to ask for help, two fellow ministers and one of our deacons came by. They sat with me for several hours until I had calmed down enough to go to bed. The deacon assured me that he 'would not let the uglies throw me out.' He even stayed the night at my house and took me to the airport the next day.

"After a ten-day visit with my family, I returned to my church. By then it was clear to me that any effort to restore my marriage would have to be long-term. My wife told me she would not be returning. When I arrived back at the church, I learned that the deacon chair and those on his side against me had been meeting and were planning to ask the church to fire me. I decided to resign and go to be with my family. Through some of the favorable deacons, I sent word that I would resign but on my terms: remain on the payroll and in the parsonage until the end of the month, continue medical coverage for my family through the end of the year. Through intermediaries I stated that if they did not accept my terms, then I would return to the pulpit, an outcome none of us really wanted.

"I returned to the church on the last Sunday of that month for a farewell service at which I did not preach. All of the opposing deacons and their families refused to attend, with one exception, the deacon chairman. His presence served as a symbol of who was really in charge. Comments from members throughout the day went like this: 'I wish this didn't have to happen; I don't know what else we can do; God bless you as you go.' Oddly, the attendance that day was one of the largest that year.

"I rejoined my family shortly thereafter and found a secular job. Many of my former colleagues from seminary days treated me as a pariah. I went for counseling at a nearby counseling center and got involved in a local church that offered me healing and compassion. In a few months, my wife filed for a divorce, having shown absolutely no interest in restoring our marriage. In recent years, I have served in an administrative position at a local major university identified with a different denomination than my own. I have never remarried, nor have I seriously considered returning to vocational ministry in spite of the encouragement of some close friends in high places in my own denomination.

"I deeply miss the pastoral and preaching side of the ministry, but I am unwilling thus far to be that vulnerable again. The life and career I dreamed about and worked toward during seminary studies have been wrecked by a group of mean-spirited people who deal with the church from an 'ownership' perspective and treat the pastor as a hireling. For them, God seems to be absent from the picture, or maybe they see themselves as delegates from God to run the church for him. I often find that my gut still clinches and I still grind my teeth when I recall these events. Hopefully in telling my story it loses a little more of its power over me."

Incidentally, Dave is one of my former students during my seminary teaching days. He is one of the brightest and best of the young ministers I helped to train for the pastorate. He is still active in a church where he now lives, serving in a volunteer role ministering to needy and deprived people. However, his life and career have been wrecked due to a small group of power-hungry antagonists in a church where he tried to be the kind of pastor they needed. He is slowly recovering, but the scars are deep. He will probably never serve in a pastoral role again.

First Nitpicky Community Church

One of the most heartbreaking letters I received came from the wife of one of my former seminary graduate students. This couple was very active and well thought of in the seminary community while in residence there. Robert earned both the master of divinity and doctor of ministry degrees while Jane, his wife, worked in one of the campus offices. At the same time, Robert was pastor of a suburban church on the outskirts of the city. A few years later I received the following letter from Jane:

"We left the seminary soon after Robert completed his D.Min. After nine years as pastor of a church near the seminary, we moved to a distant state to a typical county seat First Church. After almost five wonderful years there, Robert met with the 'buzz-saw ambush' of a bunch of deacons late one night, and they fired him on the spot. They told him that he was probably the best pastor they had ever had but that his preaching didn't fit their image of a First Church! Needless to say, it's been the most devastating walk through a heartache we have ever taken.

"Three years after it happened, Robert is still not back in a paid ministry position. We still live in the same little town (unfortunately!) and are stuck with a house that just won't sell. I came really close to a nervous breakdown over all of it and am still in the process of healing. I really wanted to take a baseball bat and beat on a few deacons and wives. You know the feeling? I guess you think I'm a pagan now!

"We hung on there to allow our daughters to graduate from high school. Our older daughter was entering her senior year as valedictorian when Robert was abruptly fired. She is now a junior honors major at a nearby Baptist college where I also work. Her sister is a freshman at another Baptist college not far away.

"I am an office manager for the school of music and was able to get scholarships for our girls. However, this job required me to move several miles away from Robert where he continues to work at a menial job and is trying to sell our house. For two years now I've had to live away from him except on weekends, but this has given me time for healing from the bitterness.

"A lot of things broke loose for me when Robert was fired. I have become very disillusioned with organized religion and the local church as it has become more social than spiritual. My father was a Baptist pastor too, and I'm just weary of everything that goes on. Yep, I've really become a pagan! It seems that God has largely been silent these last three years. I have struggled to find the 'peace that passes understanding' during this terrible time that we have lived in, so I'm having to reevaluate my concept of God and all that goes with it. Robert and I have had some struggles because he believes so much in the sovereignty of God that he has mostly waited for something to fall in his lap. I struggle between how much is the sovereignty of God and how much is our part. Needless to say, we've gone down the tube financially, as we lost two-thirds of our income with no cushion to fall back on.

"I think we will survive this experience but I will be a different person from now on. Robert is working as a janitor making minimum wage. He is depressed and discouraged and feels so abandoned by God, his peers, and the church. We've largely had to walk through this valley by ourselves. Our peers in the area just didn't provide the support we really needed. Area churches have not used Robert for pulpit supply or interim work or anything. It's hard to arrive at age fifty and literally have to start over financially, career-wise, and everything.

"I've been a very angry camper for three years now and have really struggled over the issues of forgiveness and moving on. It seems like all the things I've been taught and have taught in the church all these years just didn't measure up to reality.

"Well, the bottom line of it all at this moment is that I am trying to be thankful for the things I can: I have a good job, am loved and appreciated, have a place of ministry here in the college's school of music, and am providing an education for my children. Those are things that I can say God has not been totally silent on!

"I've been working on a letter to the local paper of the town where Robert last served. It is an attempt to educate the community on the effects of forced termination. Several churches of various denominations in this town have cruelly dismissed preachers of all ages and races. I'm sick of it and am determined to expose this process for what it is, the work of Satan. Being treated so unfairly injures real people and causes their lives to almost stop.

"We've been told our house will soon sell, and as soon as we can leave this town of small-minded, nitpicky people, we will drive by the church one more time and symbolically shake the dust off our shoes on the church property.

"I've largely quit going to church during these recent years. It's been a great freedom not to feel any obligation to have to go and be 'Ms. Hospitality' ad nauseam! I am just quite weary of the farce that organized religion has become and am continuing on a journey to really come to know God in an intimate way. I still haven't found what I'm looking for in my relationship with him but am persisting in looking. Keep us in your prayers that Robert will find a place of service to utilize his years of experience and preparation and his compassionate pastor's heart."

Robert and Jane are typical of couples who have suffered at the hands of church people. I have scores of letters in my files that read much the same. These people are not failures. They are simply abused servants of God, mistreated by "small-minded, nitpicky" lay leaders, who have no idea of how much damage they have done to these families in ministry.

Lessons from These Stories

What lessons can be learned from reading these stories and identifying with these ministers and their families? First, there are lessons for ministers who are considering an invitation from a new church:

1. Do a thorough study of the church's history, especially its manner of treating its ministers. Ask former ministers, ministers of other churches in that community, denominational leaders in the area, even a random selection of people on the street as to the church's reputation. Do as thorough a background check on the church as the pastor search committee will do on you.
2. Find out who runs the church among its lay leaders and interview them personally as to their philosophy of ministry. This will not be a large number of people. How do you find out who runs the church? Ask former pastors or staff members. Who are the five most influential members in the church, and why? Who chairs the finance committee and the personnel committee?
3. Ask to see the official job descriptions in the church's constitution and bylaws and its personnel policy manual regarding all staff positions. If they have none, watch out.
4. Ask the official board what they will do if and when someone launches an attack on the minister. If they have no strategy, either recommend one or look elsewhere.

5. Make very clear to the pastor search committee and to the official board what your philosophy of ministry is to see if there will be cooperative compatibility. If none seems likely, don't go.

6. Learn if there is a history of forced terminations in this church. If there is, you would probably be next. If you turn them down for this reason, tell them why.

7. If you are considering an old church with a long tradition, you must learn their traditions and agree to accept them or you won't last long.

8. Make sure all agreements are put in writing and inserted in the minutes of the church when the pastor search committee recommends you. Don't take anything for granted.

9. When you go to pastor a church, make and cultivate friends with the already recognized leaders. Don't try to compete with them.

10. Go with a positive attitude, smile a lot, be friendly and gracious, love the people, be a faithful shepherd, avoid negativity in the pulpit, and be a servant-leader, not a domineering leader.

11. Let them know that one of your conditions for becoming their minister is the establishment of a ministers' advisory council as described in this book. Suggest that the pastor search committee make up the initial members of this council.

There are also lessons for lay leaders of churches to learn:

1. Think about how your church has treated its minister. Be honest. Do any of the stories in this chapter sound like your church?

2. Repent of any mistreatment by your church of former ministers and pledge never to let it happen again.

3. Establish a ministers' advisory council as recommended in this book so that church bullies can be properly confronted and stopped from wrecking any minister's life and career.

4. Be patient, loving, and understanding of your ministers' actions. They are human beings just like you are. Practice the Golden Rule.

5. If you are a member of a pastor search committee and you receive an application from a terminated minister, remember the stories in this chapter and give him the benefit of the doubt. Get the facts before passing him by.
6. The future of your church will be determined largely by how you treat your ministers. Bad reputations have a long life.
7. Determine to keep your ministers a long time because successful ministers do their best work after five years.

7 Collateral Damage to Ministers

When a minister is under attack by mean-spirited people, he will not be the only one hurt. When antagonists seek to destroy a minister's life and career, the attack is like throwing a hand grenade: Several persons and relationships will be damaged if not destroyed. This can be called collateral damage.

This chapter addresses the collateral damage inflicted on a minister's marriage, children, health, peace of mind, faith, retirement, and idealism when viciously attacked by pathological antagonists and clergy killers. Human beings are much more than isolated individuals. They are part of a social system or network of relationships, beliefs, behaviors, and aspirations, including both physiological and psychological realities. When angry, power-hungry people in a church criticize, attack, or vilify a minister for reasons that cannot be substantiated with hard evidence, especially if there is no evidence of any immoral behavior or theological error, a whole host of persons and much of a minister's life and career are affected, often in a deleterious manner. Damage inflicted on a minister reaches far beyond that person's position of leadership in a church. Much more than the person's job is at stake.

Damage to the Marriage

After interviewing scores of ministers and their spouses and reading their written testimonies regarding abuse experienced in the church, there is no question that the most serious collateral damage these people have experienced is to their marriage. Obviously some of these ministers and their spouses had weak and unstable marriages before they were abused. This would be true of any category of professionals. However, many testify that until the abuse came, they had relatively strong and stable marriages. This does not mean they were problem-free. Even the best marriages have some problems. But going through ministerial abuse at the hands of a few pathological antagonists, especially when the people the minister thought were his supporters do not come to his defense, can severely impact the marriage of any minister.

Minister of Education Howard had several years of marital ups and downs. In his early thirties he was called to a church that had a history of running their ministers off. A small group of deacons ran the church in an unofficial capacity. Their leader was a very persuasive man who also happened to be the church treasurer. Usually, the night before the regular deacons' meeting, they had a meeting in one of their homes to set their agenda of control. The chairman of deacons, not one of the oligarchy, seemed naive about what was happening at the regular meeting time, but the antagonists quickly took over the meeting with their own predetermined agenda. Howard knew that something was up when the chairman would meekly set aside his own agenda for that of the troublemakers.

The treasurer, Tom, was clearly a pathological antagonist. In one of these meetings, Howard sat stunned when Tom pulled out of his briefcase a stack of phone bills and accused Howard of using the church phone to make personal long-distance calls to his parents in another city. This was all news to everyone. It was a half-truth: Howard had made some calls to his parents who were planning to host a luncheon for the youth group Howard was taking to a youth retreat several miles past Howard's hometown. It was a convenient and logical stop along the way. Howard's parents were buying and cooking all the food for Howard's youth group and their sponsors. The purpose of the calls was to make plans for the stopover. None of that mattered to Tom. These were "personal phone calls to his parents" and that was that. He said there had been other examples of church telephone abuse by Howard, but no proof was cited.

This type of harassment went on from meeting to meeting. Tom would consistently hold up or outright reject Howard's requisitions for funds for various programs, while approving those of Minister of Music Mickey, whom Tom favored. Mickey was a charmer and knew how to get anything he wanted from Tom. Furthermore, Tom knew that favoring Mickey would irritate Howard. So every time Howard requested funds for programs related to his job assignments, Tom would block these requisitions. Since the chairman of the finance committee was one of Tom's fellow antagonists, Tom could easily get away with it. Numerous similar harassment examples could be cited, but these instances of resistance began to wear on Howard. The senior pastor was in ill health and close to retirement, so he was afraid of standing up for Howard lest his own job be in jeopardy.

Howard would take his frustrations home and share them with his wife, Sue. Sue was a professional woman with a well-paying job outside of the home. Sue felt that she simply didn't have time to hear about Howard's problems. She shrugged them off as unimportant. With no sympathetic ear from his wife and no defense from his pastor or the "good deacons," Howard began to feel extremely alone.

A frustrated and angry minister can easily find himself engaged in arguments with his unsympathetic wife that can gradually become very disruptive to the marriage. When Howard found another church position in a distant city, his wife refused to go with him. They soon separated and a few months later were divorced. Howard is no longer in church work today, having decided that he could function better as a church consultant in private practice. Despite the damage to Howard's marriage and career, church treasurer Tom and the other antagonists took no responsibility for what happened.

A similar story comes from Pastor Gary, who went to lead a promising suburban church in a western city. This church also had a history of pastor-people conflicts. In over thirty years, none of their eight pastors had had a pleasant exit. Gary had received almost a unanimous vote when invited to become their pastor. However, soon after his arrival, he learned that no one on the pastor search committee was representative of the ruling oligarchy of five deacons, two of whom had long histories of disdain toward ministers. Within three years, the criticism and harassment of these few lay leaders had worn Gary down, mentally, physically, emotionally, and spiritually so much that he chose to resign and take early retirement.

Gary and his wife sold their home and moved to a distant city. Gary took a position with a church as their pastoral counselor. Early retirement meant that his income would be severely less than full employment, so his counseling work was needed to help make up the difference. When his physical and emotional health began to deteriorate further, Gary's wife, Corrine, began to withdraw from him into a world of busyness of her own making. When Gary tried to talk with Corrine about the harsh treatment at his former pastorate, Corrine refused to listen to him. The distance between them widened. Before long she refused to pray with him, saying, "Prayer is too personal"! Involving herself in the life of her elderly parents, yard work, sewing, and incessant television watching, Corrine was inadvertently taking away the only close friend Gary had left. Gary's sense of woundedness, loneliness, and rejection was too much. A friendship with another woman led to an affair that eventually resulted in a divorce from Corrine. His marriage was shattered, some of the collateral damage inflicted by church antagonists.

I have accumulated many similar stories from ministers who have been abused by churches. In nearly every case, the people most responsible for the damage to the minister's marriage consider the minister to blame. Few want to take any responsibility for the breakdown of the minister's marriage. One bitter minister whose marriage was destroyed by antagonists calls them "church sadists."

Several other wounded ministers I interviewed did not actually get a divorce, but their marriage will never be the same again. They and their wives seemingly stay together in silent pain. They have become emotionally separated. One such minister's wife considers her husband's termination from a church in effect his fault: "He should have had better sense than to accept a position with a church whose history was one of consistent conflict." She believes that God would never call a minister to a church like that. So she blames her husband for what happened. Since a divorced minister usually has a very difficult time getting a call to another church, the "emotionally divorced" minister chooses to remain with his wife even though his marriage is a very unhappy one. The damage has been done, and none of the wounding churches seems to care.

In my research, not one wounding church offered their wounded minister an opportunity, financially or otherwise, to secure marriage counseling to help the couple work through the stress they had experienced. And since medical insurance may not cover marriage counseling, the wounded minister and his wife may be on their own in securing help from professionals.

Damage to Children

When a church abuses a minister, the minister's children will be abused as well. This is especially true when the children are teenagers or young adults. Watching their father and mother being abused by callous and cruel lay leaders, a minister's children will usually become cynical about the church. Their reasoning goes like this: *You people deeply hurt our parents, often over trivial matters, and you call yourselves "Christians"! If that is Christianity, you can have it!* Bitter, disappointed, and discouraged, the children of abused clergy are inclined to leave the church, never to return.

Pastor Bob and his wife, Barbara, had three adult children who were married and lived in other cities, but they visited their parents from time to time on weekends when they had opportunity to attend worship services on Sunday in their father's church. They gradually got to know some of the people and were well aware of what was going on in Dad's church. Whether unfortunately or otherwise, these young adult children were told by their parents that a power struggle was under way in the church. A small group of deacons was trying to run their father off for trivial reasons.

These children knew their father was a good preacher and a very good pastor. He had been their pastor when they lived at home. They had heard him preach every Sunday. They could not understand what was making these deacons so mean. When the showdown came and their father chose to take early retirement and resign his position, the children were helpless to do anything about it. They had seen conflict in the church before, but this was too much. Their father was in his early sixties and had nowhere to go. How many churches would call a sixty-two-year-old pastor? He sent out his résumé but nothing opened up.

Bob and Barbara's children now concluded that church is a place where people hurt you. Why expose yourself to this kind of pain? They still considered themselves Christians and would occasionally attend a church where they lived, but serious involvement in church life stopped. They generalized that if this particular local church could treat their father this way, then any church would do the same thing. Faulty reasoning it was, but when your parents are wounded by a church, the emotional reaction overrides reason. Such children of clergy also subconsciously wonder, *Where was God? Why did he allow our father to be pressured out of the pastorate with nowhere to go?*

One twenty-eight-year-old son of a wounded minister told me the following: "When Dad was dismissed by his church, I could hardly believe it was happening. A small group of older men, all loser-types in their respective secular work experiences, decided they knew more about how to run the church than Dad, who was a veteran of many years in the ministry. I saw them crush his spirit and destroy his confidence that the church would protect him from such ruthless people. I am very bitter that this could happen to my father, a man who loved God and the church so much. I want no part of such an institution. I can find more kindness in the corporation where I work and, yes, in the local bar down the street. Why do the so-called good people in a church tolerate such behavior? I am wondering how I am going to explain to my children someday what happened to their grandfather in his last pastorate."

Damage to Health

Becoming a wounded minister can very easily become a gateway to poor health. Long-term, persistent stress can have a detrimental effect on one's physical health. This effect is often silent and undetected. Several wounded ministers have borne testimony to me of the physiological and emotional damage they experienced at the hands of ruthless pathological antagonists and clergy killers. I offer myself as a good example of this happening.

In 1984 while teaching in a graduate theological seminary I had to have triple bypass open-heart surgery. The procedure was very successful. But seven years later, as I have related, I was serving as the pastor of a heavily conflicted church led by a small group of antagonists. After several months of being blindsided by unbelievable criticism, the emotional trauma began to take its toll on my physical health.

It all seemed to come to a head on Easter Sunday of 1994. I was in the bathroom getting ready for Sunday services. Suddenly I became weak and passed out onto the floor. After my wife assisted me back into bed, I checked my blood pressure. It was dangerously low. The next day my physician described this experience as a vasovagal reaction whereby a sudden drop in blood pressure so affects the vagus nerve that one passes out. Being a very astute physician, he then asked me to describe my emotional life, both at home and at work. When I described the situation at the church, he strongly urged me to get out and do something else. Otherwise, he said, you will end up dying for those people. I chose to think of it as possibly dying "because of" those people.

Fluctuations in blood pressure, increased heart rate, sleepless nights, mental anguish, flushes of anger, feelings of total frustration and helplessness continued to take their toll on my physical health. I had never dealt with such mean-spirited people before in my life. I simply did not know how to handle them.

Some years ago pastoral theologian Howard Clinebell discussed how crises and losses are so often cumulative.[1] He referred to an article by psychiatrists Thomas H. Holmes and R. H. Rahe who had developed a stress scale of common life experiences.[2] They assigned the death of a spouse a stress score of 100; then they measured the relative stress in the lives of the persons they studied caused by other changes and losses and assigned a rating to each event. The researchers discovered that approximately 50 percent of persons with a cumulative stress score (within twelve months) of between 150 and 299 became ill in some serious way or another. About 80 percent of those with stress levels over 300 suffered some serious illness.

I applied the Holmes and Rahe scale to my own experiences. My score was 351. I was suffering from cumulative stress overload. And there were other major life stresses not on this scale that I was experiencing. No wonder my health was beginning to break!

The detrimental influence of stress on the health of one's body is well documented in psychosomatic literature.[3] The negative effects of stress on ministers in particular has also been investigated.[4] There is no doubt that ministerial training should include understanding of and constructive techniques for dealing with stress.

Lay leaders should also realize that when pathological antagonists and clergy killers are allowed to roam free in their attacks on ministers, it is as much a threat to a minister's life as is a mugger's attack in a parking lot. It is just easier for these ecclesiastical brutes to get away with their crimes against ministers. Am I being too harsh with a minister's carping critics? If the reader thinks so, then he or she needs to experience a cardiac arrest as the result of "the fiery darts" of such critics.

Damage to Peace of Mind

A minister's peace of mind is very important to the quality of his productivity in ministry. It is very difficult to be loving, gentle, and kind toward people when a small group of nitpickers are constantly at him about trivial matters that have little to do with the overall purpose of the church. It is even more difficult to be the gentle pastor, meek and mild, when the accusations leveled at him are contrived and totally false.

Most of the wounded ministers I have interviewed or corresponded with felt that the criticisms of their antagonists were unjust and unfairly propounded. In many cases these ministers were not given any kind of forum in which to answer the charges. False and unanswerable accusations that strike at the heart of the minister's integrity can be very disruptive to his peace of mind.

In my last pastorate, when an antagonist accused me, in letters to the deacon board, of flying all over the nation speaking at conferences for monetary reasons and doing so on church time, I was dumbfounded. It simply wasn't true. I could only wish that I had been that popular and earning that much extra income! But the accusation implied that I was doing this extra speaking surreptitiously and in violation of the church's personnel policies on absences from my local church duties. I could easily prove the erroneous nature of the charges, but our good but passive deacon chairman advised me to ignore the accusations. So I was left accused without rebuttal, which caused some people to wonder whether there might be some truth in the accusations. After all, these letters were written by an officer of the church and signed by five other deacons, who relied only on his word that the accusations were true.

None of these men bothered to check with me as to the accuracy of the charge. This left me very distressed and troubled. It was one of a series of charges that the antagonists kept floating among the congregation. No one came to my defense in deacons' meetings or congregational business meetings. I began to lose sleep at night. I found it difficult to concentrate on my sermon preparation. Even God seemed strangely silent in my prayer life. Standing in the pulpit on Sundays became more and more of a chore or burden, knowing that some of the people had been poisoned toward me with a wide variety of false accusations. As I preached, the antagonists would sit smugly in their pews with smirks on their faces as if taunting me to counterattack in my sermons. Mentally I became very distressed. My peace of mind was gone.

Several younger ministers have testified to me in correspondence and in conversations that they had been subjected to similar false charges and that they were finally worn down with such distractions until they either lost their tempers in public or simply resigned in despair. When a minister loses his temper in public, whether in an official board meeting or in a congregational meeting of some type, he always loses. If he just quietly resigns, most people simply do not understand and assume it was the minister's choice. They never consider the possibility that the church drove him away.

From my research regarding wounded ministers, I have concluded that there is widespread clinical depression among ministers. This is a difficult statistic to gather. Most depressed ministers would be unwilling to admit it even on a psychological test for depression. For one thing, it would be considered an admission of a weakness in their faith. Ministers already have a public image of weakness, often confused with the virtue of meekness. But the large number of ministers who leave the ministry for some type of secular work each year is one strong indication that clinical depression is at work among them. I rarely find a minister today who is truly happy in the ministry. They are either looking for a "better church" or for some other line of work.

Space does not allow me to go into a detailed discussion of depression, but it may be helpful to list the primary symptoms.

- Persistent sad, anxious, or "empty" mood
- Feelings of hopelessness, pessimism
- Feelings of guilt, worthlessness, helplessness
- Loss of interest or pleasure in hobbies and activities that you once enjoyed, including sex
- Insomnia, early-morning awakening, or oversleeping
- Appetite and/or weight loss or overeating and weight gain
- Decreased energy, fatigue, being "slowed down"
- Thoughts of death or suicide, suicide attempts
- Restlessness, irritability
- Difficulty concentrating, remembering, making decisions
- Persistent physical symptoms that do not respond to treatment, such as headaches, digestive disorders, and chronic pain[5]

If the reader can identify with half or more of these symptoms, he or she should seek a mental health professional for a thorough diagnosis and treatment. Check the phone book listings for a psychiatrist (M.D.), a clinical psychologist (Ph.D.), a clinically trained pastoral counselor (with C.P.E. certification), or a licensed professional counselor (L.P.C.) and make an appointment.

Ministers should never feel shame or guilt for seeking a mental health professional to treat their depression. One's peace of mind is very important for carrying on an effective ministry. Depression is not necessarily a sign of spiritual weakness. Stubbornly refusing to seek help for such a problem is. It is unfortunate that many wounded ministers would rather discuss their sex life than their mental health status.[6]

My friend and former pastor, C. Welton Gaddy, has written a superb autobiographical document of his own struggle with clinical depression and the long journey back to mental health. *A Soul under Siege* is must reading for all ministers who deal with this common malady. As you read Dr. Gaddy's account, you will walk with him through the labyrinth of sickness, despair, confrontation, therapy, and healing. If you will allow him, Dr. Gaddy can be your mentor, guiding you through the fog of depression to help you find the sunlight of renewal in ministry.[7]

Damage to Faith

Wounded ministers may develop a very serious problem regarding their faith in God. The most commonly asked question by wounded ministers is, Where was God when I was so viciously attacked by these pathological antagonists? Or similarly, Why does God allow clergy killers to roam so freely in the life of the church? Or, to rephrase Rabbi Harold Kushner's best-selling book of some years ago, Why do bad things happen to good people?[8]

Philosophers of religion have coined a word to deal with this problem: *theodicy,* which is an effort to vindicate the justice of God in permitting natural and moral evil. If God is both good and all-powerful, why does he allow any form of evil to exist at all? Christian philosopher Elton Trueblood has a very helpful discussion of this problem for those who want to pursue this matter further. His best answer is the simple childlike faith of the author of the Book of Job. In the end we will see that God has always been doing what is right, even if we cannot see it now.[9]

For various reasons, ministers expect God to protect his servant in the ministry from criticisms, especially from within the ranks of the congregation where he serves. Jesus warned his disciples regarding persecution (Matt. 5:10–12), and the apostle Peter alerted believers about suffering as Christians (1 Peter 3:13–20; 4:12–19). However, the implication of both Jesus and Peter was that the abuse would come from outside the church, not within. So the wounded minister reasons, *What is going on when caustic opposition comes from within the congregation?*

Several of the wounded ministers I have interviewed and corresponded with are so bitter over having been abused in the ministry by pathological antagonists and clergy killers that they have left not only the ministry but also the church. As we have seen, some of those who have left the ministry may be found on the periphery of the church, occasionally attending a local church but not active in any leadership role. Their attitude is, I will not be burned again and I will not subject my family again to the abuse we experienced—even though they have left the congregation where they were abused.

Some have told me they have even stopped reading the Bible and praying. Why? "What good did it do when I was an active pastor being chewed up by a church, and I had done nothing to deserve that kind of treatment?" They reason that if God cannot protect them from such harsh treatment at the hands of a church, then why would he bother to listen to their prayers? Or worse, if God would not protect them from church abuse, then why would he be worthy of the prayers and devotion of sincere ministers? Why pray to such a weak deity?

Another problem wounded ministers face is the attitude of a new church they are attending. A terminated minister is often looked on as a sort of pariah, a victim of ecclesiastical leprosy. Some wonder if something is wrong with him. Why was he terminated by his former church? Some people often assume the worst rather than learn the truth. All ministers know that if you are not an active minister in a recognized position, it is very difficult to find another position because of the questions that are raised in the minds of search committee members. They reason, "If he was fired, then he must have done something terrible." This also makes it difficult even to attend another church. Such ministers feel like outcasts and easily identify with the lepers in the Bible who had to announce their presence with the words, "Unclean, unclean" (Lev. 13:45–46). If a person is rejected in one church, it is very difficult to be accepted in another. It is nearly impossible to rid oneself of the "rejected" label in some church circles.

The result may well be the loss of the minister's faith. In nearly every town or city you will find one or more bitter and cynical former ministers who were abused by some congregation. They are the walking wounded. They do not need condemnation. They need healing and restoration to ministry. Mentally, spiritually, and emotionally healthy laypersons and ministers in church leadership positions need to identify and reach out with healing love to these wounded ministers whose faith has been severely damaged.

Damage to Retirement

Even wounded ministers will some day need to retire with a livable income. For many years ministers try to accumulate enough retirement investments from which to derive a livable retirement income in their mid- to late-sixties. Nearly all major denominations have such a retirement program in cooperation with the local churches' contributions on behalf of their ministers. Usually the ministers also contribute.

However, any forced termination will usually halt the contributions from the local church, and if the minister's income stops at that time, his major concern is immediate survival, not his retirement contributions. Therefore, the halting of a minister's income will inevitably affect his anticipated retirement income. This is especially true of a minister terminated during his fifties and early sixties, usually his peak time of income production and retirement contributions.

This happened to me when I was pressured out of my last pastorate at age sixty-two and forced to take early retirement. This resulted in an income of much less than I had been anticipating. Furthermore, this resulted in my having to continue working more years than I had expected. I am currently sixty-nine and still having to work to maintain a comfortable standard of living. How long I can keep this up I do not know. If I could have stayed in the pastorate another five to ten years, I could have retired without financial anxieties regarding the future.

The pathological antagonists who led the charge to get rid of me could not have cared less about my retirement income. They felt fully justified in their actions: They believed they were doing God's work for him. The passive good folks who allowed my termination to take place thought that a three-months' severance package would make up for any financial loss to me. It never occurred to them that I had several productive years ahead of me and that taking early retirement would prove costly to me in the long run.

The several wounded ministers I have been in contact with all testify to the same experience: The abusing church has no compassion regarding their former minister's retirement. The damage they inflict goes uncompensated. These churches are very fortunate that wounded ministers do not usually secure the services of an attorney and sue them for damages. One sympathetic layman advised me to take these pathological antagonists to court to put a stop to this type of "nonsense" as he called it, especially since I had considerable documentation in my possession to prove both slander and libel. But what minister of the gospel really wants to do this? The time and expense of a lawsuit would be devastating in more ways than one. I simply did not have the emotional energy to do it. Also, my more immediate concerns were financial survival, which resulted in my moving to a distant city. In addition, the reputation of a wounded minister who sues people in a church will usually be adversely affected.

Some readers may be thinking of Paul's admonition in 1 Corinthians 6 against believers taking other believers to court. But ministers who have been wounded at the hands of pathological antagonists and clergy killers will invariably question whether those people are truly believers in Jesus Christ. If you have ever been on the receiving end of such vicious attacks, you will know what I mean. This is also the reason I strongly recommend each church's having a ministers' advisory council with clout from the church to deal with antagonists. Otherwise the church leaves the wounded minister with no other recourse than to resign and silently leave or to dig in, unless he is willing to take such ruthless people to court.

Damage to Idealism

Most ministers are persons of high ideals regarding both themselves and the church. An ideal is a standard of perfection, beauty, or excellence. Ministers of God and of the church, by their very nature, enter and engage in ministry with an idealistic approach to the work of the church. They tend to be somewhat perfectionistic about the nature and work of the church. A minister envisions his church as full of loving people who deeply care about others, both in and out of the church. Therefore, church people should not be self-seeking or greedy for power. Church leaders should embody the ideals of the Christian life in all of their behavior. Church problems should be solved through rational discussion, compromise consensus, prayer, and compassion. Ministers and official church lay leaders should work together in harmony and cooperation, not discord and conflict.

However, over a period of time, a few pathological antagonists and clergy killers can sow discord and instigate conflict throughout the congregation, so much so that the minister's idealism can be tragically shattered, and sometimes damaged beyond repair.

This is especially the case if a minister experiences this type of conflict in more than one church early in his ministry. Unfortunately, sequential conflict in two or more churches causes the minister to conclude that all churches are this way.

Damaged idealism happened to me in my last pastorate and to nearly all of the wounded ministers I have interviewed or corresponded with in my preparation for writing this book. Looking into their faces, hearing their comments, or reading their words of correspondence, it is clearly evident that their idealism about the church is all but gone. The harsh facts of reality have set in, even to the degree of making cynics out of them. Most of us are bitter, angry, disillusioned, and discouraged to the point that we will probably never serve in a place of ministry leadership in a church again.

Most wounded ministers suffer from clinical depression as a result of the abuse they have experienced. It is virtually impossible to be idealistic about the church and be depressed at the same time.

Usually ministers describe their going to assume a position in a church with excitement and joyful expectation. Their vision for the new church position is pregnant with enthusiastic possibilities. Their idealism runs high. But by several months later, after being chewed up in the ecclesiastical meat grinder of internal church politics led by mean-spirited and greedy power mongers, even though only a few, the initial idealism will have been shot to pieces. Is this what church work is all about? Why don't the people who called me have high ideals and an exciting vision for the church's future? Why have I been rudely awakened from a wonderful dream, finding that I have moved from a dream to a nightmare?

When I went to my last pastorate, I was fifty-nine years old, so I knew that it would probably be the final pastoral assignment of my ministry. I began my work there with considerable excitement. My vision statement was exactly what they wanted to accomplish. The deacons pledged their full support to me. The attendance was excellent. The logistics of making a move were expedited smoothly and quickly. It seemed that God was confirming my call in a variety of ways. But in less than six months, I began to realize that I had made a mistake. The "uglies" began to show their heads by challenging my leadership at nearly every turn. None of them had been on the pastor search committee and were not actively engaged in the arrangements to bring me in as pastor. But I discovered that they were the real movers and shakers of the administration of the church. I could do little if anything without their approval.

By the end of the first year I realized that my ministry would in all likelihood be a repeat of the conflicted history of the church, a history that had been kept from me in the beginning. Within two years I was being harassed at every turn. The small oligarchy of five deacons was making it clear to me that they ran the church. Before long, my idealism about the church was gone.

What Can Be Done

To those readers who may be among the pathological antagonists in your church, I have this to ask of you. Realizing the collateral damage that you are inflicting on your minister, his marriage, his children, his health, his peace of mind, his faith, his retirement, and his idealism, why are you doing this? Why do you want to inflict this kind of damage? Why do you want to hurt someone so much?

To those readers who may be among the so-called good but passive lay leaders in your church who are standing aside and allowing the pathological antagonists and clergy killers to inflict such massive damage on a person and his ministry, I simply ask, Why are you allowing this to happen? Why are you not doing something to stop this nonsensical cruelty? Why do you not care what happens to your minister?

The Head of the church once commanded, "Do unto others as you would have them do unto you." Put yourself in the abused minister's place. Exercise some simple empathy. Feel his pain. Now do something courageous about it. Stand up for him, speak out on his behalf, initiate the organizing of a ministers' advisory council as recommended in this book, confront any antagonistic lay leaders with firmness, and let the entire church know that you as one member will no longer tolerate any further abuse of your minister. Volunteer to be his "spiritual body guard!"

To the minister, there are things you can do to prevent and/or recover from collateral damage. I offer the following recommendations based on the lessons I learned during those days. See part 3 for more extensive information on what can be done.

1. If your marriage is weak or battered, get professional counseling from a certified pastoral counselor who understands the stresses on a minister's marriage. Whatever the cost, do it. Your medical insurance may cover this if your family physician will refer you to a counselor. If your marriage has already failed, you will undoubtedly need professional counseling to help you deal with the pain, guilt, frustration, and feelings of hopelessness regarding your future in ministry.

2. Encourage your children to get into family counseling for themselves, preferably with a certified pastoral counselor. They also need to deal with the pain and anger that follows in these circumstances. If your children are still living with you, consider including them in family counseling.

3. Work closely with your personal physician to protect your health. Develop a professionally designed diet and exercise program, including stress management counseling.

4. Learn everything you can about clinical depression and don't be ashamed to take antidepressant medication, if prescribed, since depression largely has medical roots.

5. Initiate setting up a ministers' and wives' support group among fellow ministers in your town or area that will meet regularly. This group may be led by a professional counselor who is a committed Christian. See chapter 14 for specific guidelines on how to do this.

6. Start planning for your retirement *early* in your career and never withdraw from the corpus of your investments for other purposes.

7. Let your ministers' advisory council run interference for you against all major problems in the church. Garner their support and follow their wisdom.

8 Collateral Damage to the Church

When ministers are wounded by certain leaders in the church, those ministers and their families are not the only ones who suffer collateral damage. The church itself will be severely damaged in several ways. For every wounded minister, there will also be in time a wounded church. It is very costly in more ways than one for a church to abuse its ministers.

I know of no published statistics regarding the amount of collateral damage to churches in conflict.[1] My research is based largely on anecdotal testimonies provided by wounded ministers who were pressured out of their church by an antagonistic oligarchy. I have also interviewed several lay leaders of churches that terminated their minister. And finally, my conclusions are based on my own personal experience and observations.

Evangelism

When a minister of a church is abused by an oligarchy of antagonistic lay leaders (or when a staff minister is abused by an antagonistic pastor), the word about the conflict inevitably gets out to the community served by the church. Unchurched people eventually learn that this is a church that abuses its ministers, and this is something they can't understand. They wonder: *Is this the way Christians treat their leaders? Why do they behave in such an unkind, unloving manner?*

Therefore, a major casualty of minister abuse is the church's evangelistic outreach. Why would non-Christians want to associate with, much less join, such a group? And if there are new converts being brought into the church, many of them will not remain in a conflicted and abusing congregation for long.

In my last pastorate, I served for three and a half years. During that length of time, we baptized 82 converts, most of whom were adults, and had 144 additions by transfer for a total of 226 new members. I personally led a large percentage of the new converts to Christ myself.

However, the attendance did not grow proportionately. Because of the antagonists, retention of many of the new members was almost impossible. Even though most of the new members were attracted to our church through my personal and pulpit ministry, with the help of a few of our lay folk who were willing to visit in homes, many chose to leave after a few months because of the critical spirit of the half dozen antagonists and their spouses.

When the two top antagonists were both present during the worship services, one could literally feel the quenching of the Spirit. It seemed that there was nothing I could do about it. These men often glared at me during the sermon with cynical smirks on their faces. It took all the grace I could muster to ignore them. There were times after the worship services when these men would confront me with their antagonistic comments. I recall on more than one occasion some new converts and some prospects standing nearby and overhearing what they said to me. No wonder the newcomers soon left the church, never to return.

Abusive lay leaders (as well as pastors) can quickly kill any evangelistic spirit in a church. Then, of course, when people leave, who gets blamed? The minister, naturally. He is blamed for the decline in evangelism. Telling the clergy killers what the departing members gave as their reason for leaving makes no difference. Antagonists are always "right." Loss of members, contributions, and spiritual fervor is, for these self-appointed judges of the ministry, always the minister's fault.

Yet as I surveyed the list of new members during these nearly four years, it was clear that not one new convert or new member joined our church as a direct result of the witness of these antagonists. Rather, they were driving people away. I kept asking myself, *Why do they want to do this? Why do they want to kill the spirit of evangelism in our church?*

Among the several wounded ministers I have surveyed, the same story is being repeated. Churches that abuse their ministers are not growing churches. They either stagnate or eventually die, if not in numbers, at least in spirit. The church I left six years ago, located in a booming metropolitan area with tremendous potential for growth all around them, has never recovered its evangelistic spirit, lost in the midst of conflict. Some of the antagonists have left the church, some moved out of town, some have died, but others remain and continue to contaminate the unsuspecting and naive.

Financial Contributions

When a church tolerates the abuse of a minister, it will cost the church also in financial contributions. One can measure the degree of abuse by the decline in offerings. This was the experience in the last church I pastored.

Before my arrival, a one-year interim period saw the financial contributions remain in a stable condition, even though many of the people were still very distressed over the way the former minister was terminated. These people continued to attend and contribute financially to the church, hoping that the situation would be different when a new minister arrived.

Yet during my first year of tenure, criticisms began to emerge. So when the people who had stayed in the church to see what things would be like with a new minister began to realize that nothing had really changed, they decided to leave and join other churches in the city. Within a year about one hundred regular attenders and contributors had left. Naturally the financial contributions dropped significantly.

The leading antagonist, a deacon, weekly and sometimes daily called the financial secretary to monitor the financial status of the church. When the offerings began to decline, he called other influential members of the church with alarming reports of what was happening. Who did he blame? You guessed it: the new pastor. The antagonist's accusations were general and vague: The pastor's sermons are too intellectual and are not what people need to hear; he doesn't spend enough time in his office; he doesn't visit enough; when the pastor speaks, it's not so much what he says as it is the way he says it; people are leaving the church because they do not like the pastor. The criticisms were nonspecific and unanswerable.

I am reminded of the story of Jesus' trial before Pilate. When Pilate asked the crowd what he should do with Jesus, they responded, "Crucify him!" I sometimes wonder who the first person was to shout those words. Whoever it was started a wave of judgment that caught up the entire crowd. In the movie *Ben Hur*, a certain little wiry fellow had earlier portrayed Satan in several scenes. In the scene before Pilate, the camera zooms in on that same fellow who is standing out in the crowd as he becomes the first person to shout "Crucify him!" In dramatic fashion, the author of *Ben Hur*, Lew Wallace, sought to identify Satan (the word means "the accuser") as the prosecutor at Jesus' trial, the impetus behind the plot to get rid of Jesus.

The antagonist in my church functioned in a similar way. On one occasion when I was in that man's home trying to win his support, the phone rang five times—calls from church members. I could hear only the deacon's side of the conversations, but it was clear that these calls were from people whom this deacon had earlier called about "the condition of the church." It was obvious that he had been stirring up members of the church over "the pastor's causing a decline in financial contributions."

The drop in offerings made a lot of the people in the church very nervous. Why? In earlier years the church had constructed a new building, and the monthly mortgage payment was more than $14,000 out of monthly income of about $33,000. The remaining $19,000 had to be tightly stretched to cover all of the other expenses: salaries, operational items, missions contributions, and so on.

Since it is much easier to blame the minister for a decline in financial contributions than it is to blame a small antagonistic group of longtime lay leaders, the minister will usually bear the brunt of the criticism. This same process is true in national politics: If the economy is good, the president is responsible, but if the economy is bad, the president is also responsible. So many people are fickle and simplistic when it comes to cause and effect.

Few members of the church realized that the real cause of the decline in financial contributions was due to the turmoil stirred up by the antagonistic oligarchy. When good and decent laypersons allow such a group to trouble the fellowship of a church and "crucify" its minister, it will nearly always cost them financially. At first, the minister is blamed for this situation. Only after he is abused and expelled will some thinking people be able to look back and recognize what was really happening. Unjustly and unfairly abusing a minister is a very expensive endeavor in a church.

Attendance

It stands to reason that when a church allows one or more of its ministers to be abused by pathological antagonists over a period of time, it will cost that church not only the loss of evangelistic zeal and financial contributions but also its weekly attendance. Of course, there will always be a core of loyalists who will attend "their church" no matter what some leaders are doing to their ministers. Many simply turn a deaf ear and pretend the problem doesn't exist. But many more will gradually stop attending, if for no other reason than out of protest over the abuse they see taking place. Before long, many will feel so disgusted over the oligarchy's abuse of the minister that they will leave the church permanently and join another church.

As I said earlier, this happened in my last pastorate when the abuse began to be more and more public. Many of those who stopped attending our church had joined during my ministry there. They felt a certain natural loyalty to me, especially if I had baptized them. But they also felt like outsiders as far as the decision-making body of deacons was concerned. They felt helpless. These newer members could not easily infiltrate either the deacon board or any of the more powerful key committees that ran the church. Those positions were systematically recycled among the same people year after year. Newcomers to the congregation were always "suspect" to the old-timers in power.

By my second year in that church, I began to notice a gradual dropping away of several persons and families. Those I learned about I contacted as soon as possible. They all said the same thing: We cannot stay in a church where there is so much criticism and conflict, especially that which was aimed toward the pastor. Several elderly members told me that at their age they felt the need to be in a church where there was peace and harmony. Therefore, in less than four years, the attendance dropped from 400 plus to 200 plus, at the same time that we had approximately 226 additions. Naturally, some losses were due to death and moving out of town, but most of the losses were the result of the abusive tactics of the oligarchy who kept challenging the pastor's leadership.

The testimonies of the wounded ministers I have surveyed all reveal the same tendency of decreasing attendance with one sad exception: When the conflict becomes public, many irregular attenders begin showing up in unusual numbers, especially at congregational business meetings when the conflict is likely to be part of the agenda. I am reminded of an observation I often made as a boy in my hometown neighborhood: When two dogs get into a fight, the other dogs in the neighborhood come running to see and engage in the action.

Decreasing attendance is part of the collateral damage suffered by a church that abuses its ministers. If good and decent people cannot or do not stop the abuse, they are not likely to keep attending such a church.

Joy and Zeal

It is not surprising when a church is embroiled in conflict and when it abuses its ministers, that not only will it pay a terrible price in the depletion of evangelism and growth, a loss of financial contributions, and a decline in attendance, but it will also be severely damaged in the loss of joy and zeal in the fellowship. The most obvious victims of a diminishment of joy and zeal in a church are its youth and young adults, but this loss will really affect everyone.

It is difficult to overstress the importance of belonging to a happy church. Most people can detect a joyful congregation just by walking into one of its worship services or attending one of its Bible study classes. People's tone of voice, the sparkle in their eyes, and their nonverbal body language exhibit the degree of joy among them. The joy of a congregation is very contagious. It is an absolute essential for permanent growth. Most people are strongly attracted to a joyful church. Attending such a church on Sunday helps to take the edge off the hard knocks of life that they have experienced during the week.

Zeal is often correlated with joy. If you have one, you will have the other. Zeal expresses itself in enthusiasm. It is interesting that one definition of *enthusiasm* in the dictionary is "belief in special revelations of the Holy Spirit." The word itself comes from two Greek words, *en theos,* which translates literally, "God in" you. Every church needs joyful enthusiasm in its fellowship. It characterizes a healthy congregation.

But let a small group of angry, grumpy, critical, and disgruntled people fill key leadership roles in a church and the church's ministry and future will be in jeopardy. Such a negative group will invariably turn its venom of hate on the minister. Such a pessimistic group will become the channel of Satan's accusatory spirit. This type of group is akin to that crowd in the Gospel story that shouted, "Crucify him; crucify him!" Every wounded minister knows exactly what I am describing.

All of the wounded ministers I surveyed testified that the abusive church they served had lost its joy and zeal. When godly Christians do not stand against a small group of pathological antagonists who hold their secret meetings of criticism of the minister, gather in hateful gossip sessions in the halls of the church on Sundays, and spend time making phone calls to enlist supporters of their angry invectives against the minister, any joy and zeal in that congregation will soon dissipate, and a spirit of anger and schism will prevail. This is very costly behavior. An abusive church will inevitably become a wounded church.

All of this applies equally to a church where an antagonistic pastor instigates the abuse of one of his staff ministers out of jealousy or dislike. When a good and effective staff minister is forced by a vindictive pastor to resign, there is left behind much resentment and a troublesome spirit that drives joy and zeal away.

The Church's Future

Finally, the collateral damage experienced by an abusive church includes the harm it inflicts on its future. With declines in its evangelistic outreach and growth, financial contributions, attendance, and joy and zeal, such a church will not have much of a future.

John C. LaRue Jr. calls these congregations "high-risk churches." His study reveals that "some churches can be a toxic environment for pastors and their careers." The results of this survey, referred to in chapter 3 (*Leadership*'s 1996 survey), showed that a third of all churches that forced out a minister forced the previous minister to leave also.

> The majority of ousted pastors (62 percent) was forced out by a church that had already forced out one or more pastors in the past. At least 15 percent of all U.S. churches fall into this category, having forced out two or more pastors. On average, these churches have forced out three to four pastors. Most alarming: 10 percent of all U.S. churches, having forced out three or more pastors, can be called repeat offenders. These are the churches most likely to force out the next pastor that comes along.[2]

It is quite obvious that such high-risk churches have no real future so far as being a church worthy of the biblical name. Being abusive of their ministers, these churches have in effect canceled any meaningful ministry in the community. In other words, an attack on the minister of a church is an attack on that church's future.

In my last pastorate we tried to make plans to pay off a horrendous building debt much sooner than the mortgage called for and to lay the groundwork for long-range planning for growth and expansion. However, the few pathological antagonists, who were determined to terminate the pastor, were able to embroil the entire congregation in this conflict over leadership, which derailed all plans for the future. One antagonist even accused me of bringing in a particular representative of a major fund-raising organization because, as he said, "He's a buddy of the pastor and they have probably cut a deal," implying that I would personally benefit financially. There was no such arrangement, of course, but the accusation raised a red flag of alarm that brought any future planning to a halt. The accusation was a flagrant lie, born in his own evil imagination, but it served his purpose. Six years later that church is still struggling to hold its own in membership and attendance. The collateral damage of abusive powers destroyed its future.

As I said in the last chapter, bullying a minister out of a church with underhanded, evil tactics is a lot like throwing a hand grenade at him. It may wound or kill the minister, but a lot of other people and different aspects of the church's ministry will be damaged or destroyed as well. A sad note about this is that pathological antagonists don't really care what damage they do. They do not think beyond their accusations to the effect on the church's future.

part 2

Pathological Ministers

9   Ministers Who Invite Attack

Not all wounded ministers are the victims of the abuse of lay leaders in the church, at least not directly. There are some ministers, although a small percentage of the total, who are disturbed by various pathological conditions within themselves that go untreated and invite criticism and attack. A pathological minister is one who has one or more mental, emotional, or relational problems, which severely aggravate members of the congregation. These problems will more than likely also contaminate the spiritual life of the minister, which will adversely affect his role as a spiritual leader. The contamination will be observed in the negative impact on his influence and example as a spiritual model for the community in general and the congregation being led in particular.[1]

Since most laypersons are untrained regarding psychological problems, it is quite common for most of them to fail to recognize the pathological nature of the destructive attitudes and actions of ministers with these serious personality problems. Lay leaders tend to conclude that "our minister has some serious problems, and we can't afford to allow him to disrupt the life of our church." If the problems are serious enough, efforts to terminate will likely follow. In many instances, unfortunately, the pathological minister is passed on to some other congregation.

Is Criticism Ever Justified?

Some ministers do have serious personality problems that go undetected at first but become obvious as time passes. At first the problems are subtle and elusive. But in time, congregants begin to notice one or more of the following: excessive anger in the pulpit, a deeply depressive demeanor, extreme self-centeredness, unusual perfectionistic tendencies, abnormal attention seeking, an overly controlling attitude, an overly critical or judgmental stance regarding the behavior of others, or comments revealing high levels of anxiety. Simply put, the minister does not seem to practice what he preaches, or at least what he should be preaching.

Consequently many church members may soon conclude that the minister is not above criticism when his actions, attitudes, or words tend to be disruptive to the life of the congregation. The impact of the psychological problems of the minister are first seen in such things as a high turnover of staff members and committee leadership, decreased attendance and financial contributions, and a generally pessimistic pall hanging over the congregation.

When the minister cannot seem to get along with competent and spiritually minded staff persons, when he must attend and control every committee meeting of the church, when he frowns more than he smiles, when he complains more than he inspires, when his spouse appears beaten down and depressed (maybe even stops attending church), when he must be center stage at all church meetings, when he is known for his angry outbursts, then the people of the church are going to be critical of him, and understandably so.

However, the Bible wisely sets limits on the criticism of a minister. Paul directed Timothy and the churches under his charge: "Never accept any accusation against an elder except on the evidence of two or three witnesses. As for those who persist in sin, rebuke them in the presence of all, so that the rest also may stand in fear" (1 Tim. 5:19–20). Legitimate accusations must be supported by "two or three witnesses" and must be clearly recognized as sinful behavior by the church. If these criteria are not met, Paul implies that the accuser must be rebuked for violating scriptural standards.

Paul's source for this directive was a long-existing Old Testament standard:

> A single witness shall not suffice to convict a person of any crime or wrongdoing in connection with any offense that may be com-

mitted. Only on the evidence of two or three witnesses shall a charge be sustained. If a malicious witness comes forward to accuse someone of wrongdoing, then both parties to the dispute shall appear before the LORD, before the priests and the judges who are in office in those days, and the judges shall make a thorough inquiry. If the witness is a false witness, having testified falsely against another, then you shall do to the false witness just as the false witness had meant to do to the other. So you shall purge the evil from your midst. The rest shall hear and be afraid.

Deuteronomy 19:15–20

A ministers' advisory council would offer a contemporary application of the Deuteronomic principles regarding the disposition of accusations against spiritual leaders. Churches can ill afford to allow an isolated and unjust critic to run roughshod over a minister with accusations that are unfounded.

If criticisms are ever justified, what type of criticisms would they be? Few if any would disagree that if a minister is found to be immoral in some way or teaching heretical ideas (beliefs contrary to Scripture), he should be removed from office. And there are other attitudes or actions that could disqualify a minister from serving a church. A close look at the behavior and attitudes of pathological ministers will help us identify what criticisms could be considered justifiable.

Types of Pathological Ministers

The following discussion uses both popular descriptions and clinical categories found in the DSM-IV manual (*The Diagnostic and Statistical Manual of Mental Disorders,* fourth edition, published by the American Psychiatric Association). Some of the categories I am using are so similar that they tend to overlap with certain symptoms. Exactness of description is not always possible due to the considerable variety of behaviors among humans. However, certain types of pathological ministers can be identified in a broad descriptive manner.

Are these ministers mentally ill? Certainly some are mentally ill, but others might be better described as "dysfunctional," that is, they have one or more mental, emotional, or relational disorders that severely interfere with their ministry effectiveness. For example, not every minister who loses his temper in a Sunday sermon is mentally ill or even dysfunctional, but if anger becomes a controlling factor in his preaching, especially if aimed at certain members of the congregation on a regular basis, then a serious problem exists in the personality of that minister, which has pathological consequences.

The following "types" are listed and discussed at random with no particular order in mind. The point here is that these types reveal why such ministers invite criticism and attack due to their behavior and attitudes.

The Neurotic Minister

Even though the term *neurosis* is somewhat outmoded today in psychological literature, it still conveys the idea of abnormal or outside the bounds of average. It suggests that unusual fears or anxieties prevail in the mind of the neurotic person. Even though there are certain cultural factors influencing our understanding of neurosis (for example, in some cultures, males are taught to believe that a woman during her menstrual period may have an evil influence on others and should be avoided),[2] the term does suggest an abnormal cluster of fears adversely influencing one's interpersonal relationships as well as one's sense of personal well-being.

Pastor Donald was a minister with considerable fear of attending deacons' meetings, finance committee meetings, and other potentially stressful meetings of the church. He was so neurotic about such meetings that he became emotionally paralyzed so far as his leadership role was concerned. His church was a large congregation located in a major university city. He was so afraid of college students that he assigned a special staff minister to students to assume the responsibility of preaching at the 8:00 A.M. service designated especially for these students.

On one occasion, as we were both flying back from a conference that we had attended in Chicago, Donald told me, "I am afraid of university students." It is indeed interesting that Donald had done both master's and doctoral work during seminary days; so he was no intellectual dummy. Even though well-known as an outstanding and persuasive speaker, he was nevertheless possessed by deepseated fears of preaching to the so-called intellectually astute.

During that same period of time, one of Donald's staff ministers told me that Donald would become so disturbed and fearful before the main 11:00 A.M. worship service that he would go into his office bathroom and vomit. This happened almost every Sunday.

Donald's neurotic personality eventually brought about such criticism from his lay leaders that he felt pressured to resign from his church. Over the next few years he moved from a business venture to college fund-raising to evangelism. Then one Sunday, after beginning a series of revival services in the city of his residence, following the morning worship service, he went home and committed suicide. Behavioral externals can often hide deep internal moods that are very destructive.

A neurotic minister is one who is perceiving certain situations as distressing or potentially threatening to his career status. He is still largely in touch with reality, but his fears are enduring or recurring, the roots of which are not necessarily connected with immediately identifiable stressors. His behavior is not terribly bizarre, and its cause is not demonstrably organic in nature. Such a minister may experience panic attacks in varying degrees and may require treatment by a psychiatrist or psychotherapist or both.

A neurotic minister's behavior may be classified as one or more of the following types: anxious, depressive, phobic, obsessive-compulsive, hysterical (dissociative disorder), depersonalization, and hypochondriacal.[3] A minister who persistently experiences and manifests these types of behavior is going to be vulnerable to criticism and attack. As one layman stated regarding his neurotic minister, "If he can't hear the words of the Bible, 'Fear not,' then how can he expect us laymen to hear them?" Another layperson complained, "We ordinary church members have our own fears and anxieties to deal with; we need a spiritual leader to show us some solutions."

The Angry Minister

Anger is a normal and natural human emotion. It is one aspect of the emotional armory with which God has made humans. We have been endowed with reason, volition, and emotions that enable us to survive. All of the emotions have a positive function, but if any of them is allowed to get out of control, much harm can be done to both self and others. This is especially true of anger.

Anger is normally a defense mechanism, a punitive energy, or a control force. But if the power of anger is allowed to run rampant, it can prove to be a dangerous thing. A minister who uses anger in unhealthy, excessive ways can become pathological and thereby invite criticism and attack from his parishioners. Few church members enjoy their minister yelling in anger at them from the pulpit Sunday after Sunday. He may do so thinking he is preaching in the "tradition of the prophets," condemning sin and injustice, but doing so with an attitude of judgment and condemnation rather than love and compassion will be ineffective. Judgmental anger is different from compassionate anger, which is revealed in a broken heart. Most people can tell the difference.

The story is told of a small boy who often expressed to his parents his desire to grow up to become a minister. One Sunday, after hearing a guest evangelist at church tell stories of his sordid past before his conversion and angrily denounce sin of all types, the family was driving home. The mother asked her young son if he still wanted to grow up to be a preacher. His answer was poignant: "No, I don't think so. I'm not mean enough." That is a very sad commentary on the angry minister.

Churches can often prod their minister to express angry feelings. I have "been there, done that." Jack and Jim and their group used antagonism to agitate me into saying and doing things that resulted in conflict. They tried to block every suggestion I made regarding improving the ministry of the church. They made certain that each year they were in charge of the key committees of the church where my leadership could be effectively blocked. I felt myself becoming more and more angry as time passed. My anger began to show up in some of my written articles in the weekly church paper as well as in some of my Sunday sermons.

I tried to control my feelings but their agitations proved too much.

In the numerous interviews and written testimonies I have gathered in research for this book, the problem of anger on the part of the minister turns up time and again. As a result, I have come to the following conclusions. Many ministers have legitimate reasons for anger. Often the salary and benefits are unrealistically low and unfair in light of the incomes of the lay leaders who decide on the minister's financial situation; little if any recognition is accorded the minister who spends as many as sixty hours a week on the job (for example, no recognition of the minister's anniversary, birthday, or special accomplishments); there may be a constant chorus of complaints from critical, unhappy, disgruntled, and miserable church members whose criticisms are trivial at best and if serious are often unfounded and contrived; immature church members can be very demanding of the minister's time, so much so that he has little time left to reach out to prospective members or to work with truly needy people; often he can spend much time and energy doing good work and receive only criticism in return from those who are in a position to affirm his labor.

These examples are not given to justify a minister's anger, but only to show what can and does aggravate it. Ministers, of all people, must be extremely good at anger management; they will hurt only themselves when they do show excessive anger.

I am concerned here, though, about the minister who has become pathologically angry, who learned (wrongly) at some time in his life that anger is the best way to deal with problems or problem people. This way of coping may have been learned in early childhood; the child adopted anger as his best defense whenever he felt unjustly treated or unfairly threatened. In the church such a response always proves to be counterproductive.

If a minister wants his people to be angry and critical, then all he needs to do is show anger and a judgmental spirit in the pulpit. The pulpit seems to be the best testing ground of the impact of his own emotions. If he often reveals an excessively angry disposition and is critical of his people (for example, using a lot of judgmental "you messages"), some if not many of them will become critical of him in return. If the minister communicates an angry rejection of his people, they will reject him. If the minister preaches a verbally "violent" sermon, his people will be verbally "violent" toward him in return. As the minister goes, so goes the church. Anger begets anger.

The Narcissistic Minister

The narcissistic personality disorder is one often seen among ministers. Knowledgeable and mentally balanced laypersons are quickly turned off by a narcissistic minister. Arrogant, self-centered, attention seeking, power hungry, pushy, dogmatic, bloated with self-importance, exploitative, manipulative, and insensitive, these ministers invite a lot of justifiable criticism and opposition. They lack one of the primary characteristics of Jesus himself—humility. They can be very charming but use their charm to manipulate gullible people. They can sometimes take charge of a large church or even a denomination and seemingly get away with it.

The DSM-IV lists the following criteria for the narcissistic personality disorder. Beginning by early adult life, grandiosity (fantasized or actual), lack of empathy, and need for admiration are present in a variety of situations and shown by at least five of the following:

1. A grandiose sense of self-importance (person exaggerates his own ability and accomplishments).
2. Preoccupation with fantasies of beauty, brilliance, ideal love, power, or limitless success.
3. Belief that personal uniqueness renders the person fit only for association with (or understanding by) people or institutions of rarefied status.
4. Need for excessive admiration.
5. A sense of entitlement (person unreasonably expects favorable treatment or automatic granting of his wishes).
6. Exploitation of others to achieve personal goals.
7. Lack of empathy (person does not recognize or identify with the feelings and needs of others).
8. Frequent envy of others or belief that others envy him.
9. Arrogance or haughtiness in attitude or behavior.[4]

Reverend Patrick possessed almost every one of these traits. Newly graduated out of seminary, he was called to a large university church in a southern state. In only three years he was about to be terminated by the church's lay leadership because of his extreme arrogance, when his father, who was a prominent denominational leader in another state, secured him the presidency of a college for which he had absolutely no experience. After several years the college's board of trustees asked for his resignation amid charges of spending too much time and money playing denominational politics, jockeying for prominence and power. Friends in denominational high places rescued him with a position as head of a seminary in a distant state where his arrogant behavior continued.

Patrick finally ascended to positions of power and influence in his denomination, after taking a stand for biblical inerrancy, and accusing established denominational leaders and seminary professors of "not believing the Bible." He has a long history of seeking the termination of church pastors, seminary faculty and administrators, and other key church leaders who disagree with his questionable political methods as well as his theological positions.

Several who have worked closely with Reverend Patrick for several years have told me that he has a grandiose sense of self-importance; a preoccupation with fantasies of power and success; a belief that his personal uniqueness renders him fit only for association with those of rarefied status; a need for excessive admiration; a strong sense of entitlement of position, status, and money, exploiting others to achieve personal goals; an obvious lack of empathy for the feelings and needs of others (especially those who disagree with his methods and beliefs); a frequent envy of others in his early adult years but now a strong belief that others envy him; and an extreme arrogance and haughtiness in attitude and behavior. These former associates developed an intense dislike of Reverend Patrick to say the least.

How does a minister with a personality disorder gain position, power, and status in a national denomination? People with mental disorders are not always professionally incompetent. But the narcissism of egocentric ministers invites criticism and attack.

A disturbing number of televangelists, ministers of both large and small churches, and denominational leaders exhibit many of the characteristics of the narcissistic personality disorder. Many will in time sow the seeds of their own career destruction. Their attitude and actions are quite contrary to the life and ministry of Jesus Christ, the Lord they claim to follow.

The Overly Emotional and Attention-Seeking Minister

The DSM-IV describes the histrionic personality disorder as overly emotional and attention-seeking. Sexually promiscuous ministers may fall under this category. Ministers who must always be center stage and are very jealous if others supplant them in the life of the church would also fit here.

Criteria for the histrionic personality disorder include the following: Beginning by early adult life, emotional excess and attention-seeking behaviors are present in a variety of situations, including at least five of these:

1. Discomfort with situations in which the person is not the center of attention.
2. Relationships that are frequently fraught with inappropriately seductive or sexually provocative behavior.
3. Expression of emotion that is shallow and rapidly shifting.
4. Frequent focusing of attention on self through use of physical appearance.
5. Speech that is vague and lacks detail.
6. Overly dramatic expression of emotion.
7. Easy suggestibility ([person] is readily influenced by opinions of other people or by circumstances).
8. Belief that relationships are more intimate than they really are.[5]

Even though the afflicted person is typically female, the disorder can occur in men. This person's need for approval can cause him to be seductive, often inappropriately (even flamboyantly) so. Most lead normal sex lives, but some can be promiscuous, and others may have difficulty with frigidity or impotence.[6]

Pastor Larry exhibited most of the above characteristics of histrionic personality disorder. Before becoming a minister, he had been a successful salesman for a national company. Entering the ministry in his late thirties, he had no formal theological training. He secured an unaccredited doctor's degree from a maverick theological "degree mill." Being very persuasive and charming, he had a history of leading his pastorates to build a huge church auditorium, much larger than the congregation could justify or afford, suggesting each time that he would fill the new oversized auditorium with his "dynamic" preaching, which never happened.

In each instance these churches soon found themselves in tremendous debt, causing considerable internal conflict over how to make their monthly payments on the building mortgage. Before long, Pastor Larry was having several extramarital affairs with lonely, neurotic women, most of which were kept secret at least until after he left town. His resignations were usually announced as due to a nervous breakdown, just before he would have been forcefully terminated. Leaving a large, burdensome debt in each church, he would move several states away to take his next church, only to repeat his histrionic behavior pattern. His successors had an immediate challenge of keeping the bank from foreclosing on the mortgage as well as overcoming the distrust of ministers by laypersons who deeply resented the building debt that Pastor Larry had left behind.

No wonder the "godfather deacon" of the church felt that "you can't trust preachers," after what Pastor Larry did to them. The resultant monthly building payment, which amounted to over one-third of the church's income, was such a strain on the finances that the finance committee chairman prohibited running a modest church advertisement in the city newspaper. The fallout of this histrionic pastor's ministry has left several of his pastorates in a damaged condition almost beyond repair. It is sad that naive lay leaders fell for his charming personality every time.

The Bully Minister

The bully minister enjoys throwing his weight around, especially among his staff associates. Such a minister usually has a lust for power. Some are even called tyrannical, overbearing, or domineering. They have a deep need to control others. Some have a reputation of firing their subordinates for trivial, nitpicky reasons.

In my research for this book, I received numerous stories from church staff persons (ministers of education, music, youth, and others) regarding a bully senior minister. The subject of bullying in American schools has been carefully studied and reported,[7] but nothing has been written about the bully minister. Some of these ministers may be seriously sadistic, enjoying hurting others. Some are tyrannical, deeply insecure persons who need to control others for fear their world will come crashing in on them if they're not in control. Others are power hungry, obtaining pleasure from dominating others in a chain of command. Some may have been abused during childhood and now as adults they find a way on a subconscious level to get even with their abusers in a symbolic or substitutionary manner.

In some churches, the bully minister arrives as the new pastor with the announcement to the staff that their resignations must be on his desk his first day in the office. This is a more common practice than churches would like to admit. The bully pastor then decides whom he will keep and who will leave. A careful pastor search committee will make certain in advance that this will not happen to their church staff members.

The bully minister will immediately be intolerant of any staff member who gets more attention from the congregation than he does. Ministers of music are especially vulnerable at this point. They often lead inspiring musicals, cantatas, concerts, and other musical centerpieces, especially if they are outstanding soloists that attract public attention and inspire worship. In many instances, ministers of youth likewise endear themselves to both youth and their parents for high quality work in leading innovative and creative youth programs and ministries. If the senior minister does not have this equally dashing quality in the pulpit or in pastoral care, he may feel that he is being upstaged in the eyes of the congregation. Then if he is an insecure bully minister, he will soon pressure the more popular staff members to resign their positions.

Eventually, the bully minister will agitate enough key lay leaders of the church to oppose this type of leadership. It is unusual to find a bully minister who is able to remain in a pastorate for more than four or five years. Those who do remain for long usually have very docile and easily intimidated lay leaders. May God have mercy on any staff members who serve under a bully minister. To remain in their positions, they will have to be totally subservient yes-persons.

The ADD Minister

Attention Deficit Disorder (commonly referred to as ADD) has received much attention in recent years in books, articles, and public discussions but with primary emphasis on this condition among children. Even though it was first described as early as 1902, physicians and psychologists have been using ADD as a diagnostic category only in recent years. In the early 1990s ADD in adults began to be recognized and studied with some intensity.[8] After examining the established criteria for determining that someone is an ADD person, it is my observation that some ministers unintentionally invite criticism because the characteristics of their ADD personality adversely affect their ministry.[9]

Inattention

What are the major symptoms of ADD?[10] First, there is inattention. Having a short attention span, this person has difficulty focusing on a task assignment to its logical conclusion. Like a mental butterfly, flitting from one task or thought to another, he either cannot land on anything for long or has difficulty shifting focus when reason calls for it. Two extremes may be observed: workaholism and procrastination. He either overworks a simple job assignment to the neglect of other important assignments or he lacks the motivation to get started with even one assignment.

Impulsivity

The ADD person is impulsive, failing to stop and think about what he is doing. He fails to preplan and makes many careless errors when doing a job. When a child, this person may have run into the street without looking, but as an adult he runs ahead of his supervisor without asking for permission or clearance. He might blurt out confidential information or share intimate details with strangers. He knows the rules of proper action but breaks them anyway for lack of careful thought.

Hyperactivity

As a child the ADD person was physically "bouncing off the walls" or verbally yelling out at inappropriate times and places. It was not unusual for the five-year-old son of a church staff member to run into the church office singing loudly or yelling, which disturbed the conversations of others. If the ADD child inappropriately moves too much, the ADD adult inappropriately talks too much, reflecting restlessness and impatience. Or the ADD adult appears very busy but never seems to accomplish much.

Associate Pastor Milton was unquestionably an ADD adult. He was minister of both education and music in his church. He had a charming personality, almost a constant smile, and a beautiful solo voice. But as a professional, he knew almost nothing about church-school education and even less about church music. When his pastor gave him specific assignments, he rarely carried them out to completion. He was well paid and a financial liability to the church. How did he survive? He simply charmed his way into the hearts of certain key lay leaders, especially influential women.

This church had the potential of reaching scores of young adult parents with small children, but their preschool and children's ministry was poorly organized and directed. A lot of work needed to be done. The pastor instructed Milton to give this task a lot of attention. After several months, nothing had changed. Many young couples would attend the church, but when they saw the disarray of the church-school ministry, they naturally went elsewhere. The pastor arranged for Milton to receive the help of a local church education consultant who agreed to meet with him weekly to improve the program. They met only once. Milton chose not to take advantage of this free assistance.

One day, in frustration, the pastor asked Milton what they taught him in seminary (he had a master's degree in religious education). He chuckled as he responded, "Not much!" Several teachers in both the preschool and children's departments regularly complained to the pastor about the lack of leadership. Telling him about these complaints changed nothing. In staff meetings Milton often made excuses for not presenting regular reports of his job assignments.

Milton's performance of music responsibilities was shoddy to say the least. The church knew he had little formal training in music, but before long, they realized that there were more hymns in their hymnal with which he was not familiar than hymns he knew. He had a piano in his office; so one day the pastor suggested he take some time each week to learn some new hymns. He never did. He was one of those fellows who never accomplished much but knew how to get by with his charm.

Milton had most of the characteristics of an ADD adult. He had difficulties with attention and focusing; his activity level (people thought he was lazy); impulsivity; hyper-sensitivity; organization of time, details, and paperwork; and with his temper (especially when a church-school teacher complained to him about his lack of leadership). When under stress, Milton would take off on a work-day without permission and take his wife to a movie. The pastor simply could not depend on him to be where he was supposed to be and do what he was supposed to do.

ADD ministers need to be understood, cared for, and encouraged to seek professional help. They need to be properly diagnosed by a psychologist who is specially trained to test for ADD. The psychologist will then refer this person to a medical doctor for possible medical treatment, possibly a prescription for Ritalin (methylphenidate), which has proved to be one of the most helpful medications in stabilizing a person's brain activity.[11] But it is important to realize that ADD persons are not "sick" people, as in the sense of a mental illness. Their brain wiring is simply different than for the rest of us, and they need special medical and psychological treatment to normalize their behavior patterns. Recent research has detected a specific gene that could be the cause of this condition.[12] ADD ministers do not need to be criticized, attacked, or terminated. When churches and ministerial staffs try to understand ministers with ADD, harmonious and productive relationships can develop.[13] Yet this requires a cooperative effort on the part of the minister, who should get medical treatment.

There may well be other ways to describe the various types of pathological ministers who attract criticism. We could have developed categories that include deep insecurities, clinical depression, sexual addictions, perfectionism, "empire builders" with strong egocentric ambition, and "martyrs." But the above categories seem sufficient to illustrate how some ministers can create their own problems by their pathological tendencies.

Possible Causes of Pathology

There are several possible causes of pathological conditions that result in the behavior of ministers that attracts justifiable criticism. Of course, each behavior problem has its own unique roots, but several possibilities need to be examined. The following list is suggestive.

1. *Poor or inadequate socialization.* Socialization is the process of becoming a functioning human being, most of which takes place in the context of the person's family environment. Some pathological ministers experienced poor or inadequate socialization. For example, they may have learned more about competition or conflict than they did cooperation in family interaction. Or they may have learned to use anger as the best method to get their way. Poor social skills learned in childhood will probably result in all kinds of conflict in the adult years. A spoiled child may likely become a demanding adult. A child who developed a V.I.P. (very important person) syndrome will probably expect to be center stage as an adult. A selfish child will in all likelihood become a selfish adult. An insecure child may become an adult who always feels threatened and may use anger to protect himself.

2. *Abuse in childhood.* Related to the above, when a child has been severely abused during his early developmental years, he is more likely to become an abusing adult. Ministers who were abused in childhood often become bullies, tyrants, even sadistic adults. They may hold a core belief that says, *I was hurt by others as a child; now I will get my revenge and hurt others.* The childhood abuse may have been physical, sexual, emotional, verbal, or neglect.

3. *Unresolved anger.* Humans can learn an angry lifestyle quite early in life. Being a defense mechanism, anger may be a response to any perceived threat. If a minister often observed his father abuse his mother physically or otherwise, he may

as an adult choose to be verbally abusive to men in his church who remind him of his father. That is, he projects onto others what he continues to feel about his father. A deacon once wrote me a scathing letter because, as he said, "You remind me of my domineering father." This was the only time in my life I had ever been accused of being domineering. Unresolved anger out of one's childhood can contaminate one's adult relationships. Some have called this "unfinished business out of one's childhood."

4. *Deep-seated insecurities.* Fearful feelings out of one's past may continue to haunt one's present and future. Deeply rooted insecurities out of one's childhood may cause one to respond to stressful situations in ways that are counterproductive. Present circumstances may turn on these old "tapes" of insecurity and result in either fight or flight. Insecure ministers do not usually stay with any church for very long. They have a core belief that says, *If life gets rough, you run.* Another possible core belief might be: *If someone disagrees with you, you redefine that person as an enemy.* This can create serious problems for a minister in a church where some people are bound to disagree with him at times. Also, since insecurity is a form of fear, these fears may become the fuel that feeds inappropriate outbursts of anger.

5. *Conditional love.* If a person happened to be raised in a home of conditional love, he probably never felt really loved because he never was able to meet all of his parents' conditions. Some may even enter the ministry subconsciously in the hope of finally gaining their parents' love and approval. These people are love-starved because of their being conditionally loved in their early childhood home. This type of background can create all kinds of relational problems in adulthood. Some such ministers enter the ministry expecting the church to be that family that will love them unconditionally. If that doesn't happen, discouragement, anger, and depression will likely follow. Quite often a pathological minister is a discouraged minister.

6. *Overcontrolled childhood.* Some pathological ministers were raised in a home with one or both parents who were overcontrolling. A domineering mother is usually the culprit.[14]

Such parenting tends to rob a child of two very necessary ingredients for maturity and stability: freedom and taking responsibility for oneself. Under these circumstances deep-seated resentment may develop that persists into adulthood and can spill over into a minister's behavior in a variety of pathological ways.

7. *Alcoholic or drug-addicted parents.* Pathological ministers often reveal that they had alcoholic or drug-addicted parents (one or both) when growing up. The damaging effects of such a family life are widely observed in clinical practice. The fear, insecurity, anger, and continued resentment felt by these children continues long into adulthood.[15]

8. *Chronic physical and medical problems.* Some pathological ministers may be struggling with chronic physical or medical problems that may have never been detected or diagnosed by a physician. The possible genetic causes of ADD discussed earlier illustrate such a situation. Some ministers may struggle with clinical depression, which may be due to low levels of serotonin, norepinephrine, and acetylcholine, important neurotransmitters in the chemistry of the brain.[16] Pathological ministers could be battling migraine headaches, cardiovascular disease, sexual dysfunction, cancer, or visual problems. Chronic sickness, such as respiratory problems, allergies, and one of the major occupational hazards of a minister, losing one's voice for various reasons, could also be a factor in the pathological behavior of a minister. Chronic medical problems can be quite aggravating to a minister who believes he should be perfect.

9. *Burnout.* Brooks Faulkner has given us the best discussion of the problem of burnout for ministers in his book *Burnout in Ministry.* Burnout is physical, emotional, mental, and spiritual exhaustion that results from a human being trying to be Superman in his or her vocation. Burnout could be called career exhaustion that results from failing to recognize the limitations of one's humanity. Oftentimes ministers experiencing burnout will behave in ways that turn people against them. Just as a misbehaving child is a discouraged child, so a burned-out minister can be a mis-

behaving minister who does things that cause his people to criticize him.

Sometimes, burnout is an expression of clinical depression. The DSM-IV classifies this as a depressive personality disorder:

> The depressive cognitions and behaviors include a persistent and pervasive feeling of dejection, gloominess, cheerlessness, joylessness, and unhappiness. These individuals are overly serious, incapable of enjoyment or relaxation, and lack a sense of humor. They may feel that they do not deserve to have fun or to be happy. They also tend to brood and worry, dwelling persistently on their negative and unhappy thoughts. Such individuals view the future as negatively as they view the present; they doubt that things will ever improve, anticipate the worst, and while priding themselves on being realistic, are considered by others to be pessimistic. They may be harsh in self-judgment and prone to feeling excessively guilty for shortcomings and failings. Self-esteem is low and particularly focused on feelings of inadequacy. Individuals with this disorder tend to judge others as harshly as they judge themselves. They often focus on others' failings rather than their positive attributes, and they may be negativistic, critical, and judgmental toward others.[17]

Ministers experiencing burnout have worn themselves out (overloaded their circuits), trying to be all things to all people at all times in all situations, an impossible goal for any human being. Such persons will inevitably attract criticism from many in a congregation, especially those who do not understand what is happening to their minister. Such ministers need treatment at the hands of a competent therapist who will work in consort with medical specialists.

If the reader recognizes himself in any of these causes of pathology, you are urged to find a competent pastoral psychotherapist or a therapist with sympathies toward the ministerial profession and get help immediately.

Ministering to and Healing for the Pathological Minister

I suggest a fourfold strategy for ministering to and healing for the pathological minister. There must be awareness, diagnosis, therapy, and encouragement and protection.

Awareness

Pathological ministers must know they have a major problem that needs immediate treatment. If you have recognized yourself somewhere in this chapter, it was not written to condemn you but to help you. The tragedy of most pathological ministers is that they do not believe they have a problem of any sort. They practice denial to the utmost. Their problems, they think, are caused by others, whom they are quick to blame.

However, if you are hurting, remember that pain, even emotional and relational pain, is symptomatic of some deeper problem. Treating only the symptoms, for example, getting rid of a staff member or maneuvering a critical lay leader out of office, will not solve the problem in the long run, if the problem is resident in you.

Awareness of the minister's problem by both lay leaders and the minister is the beginning step toward solution of conflict issues and the resulting criticism.

Diagnosis

Professional help is usually needed to diagnose the nature of a minister's suspected pathology. Such help could come from a clinically trained pastoral counselor, a psychiatrist who is sympathetic to religion in general and church life in particular, a clinical psychologist who has empathy for ministers, or even an experienced older minister who has considerable wisdom from working with troubled ministers over the years (and who is knowledgeable concerning professional referral resources).

There are several psychological tests available from many therapists that a minister could take to assist in diagnosis. Two that are widely used are the Minnesota Multiphasic Personality Inventory (MMPI) and the Basic Personality Inventory (BPI). Either of these can be administered by most licensed professional counselors. Both tests are highly respected by professionals and have proved to be helpful in identifying pathological conditions in one's personality.[18] Of course, there are several other equally valuable personality assessment tests with which most therapists are familiar.

If the minister reader is aware of some personal pathological conditions, then for your own sake, for the sake of your family, and for the sake of your church, get help immediately. Be brave enough to admit that you need help. God has someone to help you who is professionally competent and who will keep the matter confidential. For the sake of the kingdom of God, don't just leave your current church situation and transfer your problems to another church. This would not be fair either to you or to the churches.

Therapy

Therapy is the professional term for finding out what is wrong and doing something constructive to correct the problem. Moreover, therapy is a process of healing for a pathological condition. Ministers who tend to create problems in their churches seldom take a hard look at themselves. They are sometimes prone to live in denial that they could somehow be responsible. Engaging in a process of therapy will enable a pathological minister to carefully examine the facts and feelings regarding the problems in his life and ministry. The therapy process could take several weeks or several months, depending on the depth of the pathology.

Psychotherapy is actually "talk therapy" whereby a person seeks to find understanding, support, encouragement, and healing for the overwhelming and debilitating problems of life. In an atmosphere of empathy, trust, and confidentiality, the counselee is guided by the therapist to use new insights to make fresh commitments regarding healthy change in both emotions and behavior. Without therapy, most pathological ministers will never change.

Encouragement and Protection

Ministers with emotional and behavioral problems do not need condemnation and rejection. They need encouragement—lay leaders and other ministers reaching out to them in love and guiding them into therapy. These wounded men and women of God need to know that someone loves them and cares about them and their future in ministry.

However, encouragement does not mean coddling them or urging them to believe that the problem will work itself out and that their critics are just cruel and merciless. Encouragement is rooted in reality, not fantasy or self-pity. Encouragement, therefore, can be painful because it forces the recipient to face up to the facts of his pathology. Many pathological problems have an addictive element, and it is very difficult to break the power of an addiction. But persistent encouragement from lay leaders and other ministers, along with a loving and redemptive attitude and help in finding the right therapist, is often what is needed to bring about a successful result.

In addition, a minister who is striving to overcome pathological personality problems needs protection from any "wolves" who would destroy him. Often Christians have zero tolerance for pathological ministers. They have no patience, no mercy for the afflicted minister. Here is another place for a ministers' advisory council to step in and function effectively to redeem a difficult situation. Churches must stop shooting their own wounded.

I would simply ask any lay readers of this book to go back and reread the above section on causes of pathology. If you were so afflicted, how would you wish to be treated? I recall that Someone once said, "Do unto others as you would have . . ."!

10

Abuse from Pathological Ministers

Some of the saddest stories regarding wounded ministers have to do with pathological ministers who abuse their own staff ministers in one way or another. In gathering information and stories in preparation for writing this book, almost 50 percent pertained to staff ministers who were abused by their senior minister. This is not a scientific statistic but it surely was distressing to learn that so many were wounded by their own pastor.

Senior ministers who abuse their staff ministers seem to fall into the category of the pathological ministers discussed in the previous chapter; at least a large percentage would be so classified. We could discuss several types of abuse but the following story is illustrative of this behavior.

Associate Pastor Tom

Tom had served as pastor of a church prior to his second assignment, which was to be the associate to an older minister in a larger church with more ministry potential. This is his account: "I had served in the same county as Pastor Charles and thought I knew him fairly well when he asked me to become his associate. However, within a short time he had turned from Dr. Jekyll into Mr. Hyde. I lasted less than one year before God rescued me in order to save my sanity.

"Pastor Charles had created a new position for me with no specific job description, which should have been a warning to me. What Charles told me I would be doing was different from the church's expectations of me. A few weeks after I began my ministry, I met with the personnel committee to define my job description. They told me it was two words: 'Help Charles.' In other words, whatever Charles wanted me to do, I had to do, and the church would go along with it.

"Charles was a workaholic and a visitation fanatic, and he decided I should be just like him. Two months into my ministry he told me I had to make a minimum of twenty-five visits per week, split between inreach and outreach. To keep me accountable, every Monday morning I had to turn in to him the names of the persons or families I had visited the previous week. He said that he sometimes made visits late into the evening, and I should do the same also. His bottom line was this: 'You do whatever it takes to make your visits and bring people into the church.' To drive home this point, he told me that if I led someone to Christ, I could baptize that individual, but if he led someone to Christ, then he would perform the baptism. The church found out about this, and of course it was perceived as a contest between Charles and me. Most months I 'lost,' and I was publicly embarrassed.

"Charles also had some strange ideas about ministry to families. He believed that we had a ministry responsibility toward a person who was a family member of someone in our church, even if that person was actively involved in another church. He often sent me to the hospital to visit members of other churches, and sometimes I had to attend funerals of members of other churches who were only distantly related to members of our church. I especially felt silly doing this when I entered the hospital room and found the person's pastor present, providing pastoral care. I could only count these visits against my twenty-five if the person was a church member or a prospect for church membership. Charles kept me accountable for these uncountable visits also, by orally asking for reports. These accountability tactics became abusive because I knew that if I didn't meet his expectations (which often changed), then I would get yelled at (literally!).

"Visitation and other duties were already filling up my time each week when, about four months into my ministry, Charles told me that he was requiring me to attend each committee meeting that took place in the church. Sometimes he was there; sometimes he wasn't. If he wasn't present at the meeting, of course, I had to give a full report to him. He also felt that since there was no minister of education at the church, I should assume those responsibilities too. He required me to have regular Sunday school leadership meetings on top of everything else.

"Six months into my ministry I was desperately burned out. I felt that I was being treated like a slave. Charles never expressed appreciation for my work. Like Pharaoh, he kept telling me I had to make the same number of bricks as before, only now I had to gather my own straw. Whenever I didn't make the visitation quota or meet some other expectation, I got yelled at for not working hard enough. Charles was a large man with a loud voice; he could intimidate Attila the Hun. The verbal abuse took place just often enough to keep me 'walking on eggshells.'

"I began looking for any way out. I wasn't sleeping well, I was in constant fear of Charles, I had no free time, and worst of all, I knew it wasn't ever going to get better unless I left. What disgusted me most was that Charles was two-faced. He was charming in public, but generally he acted like a tyrant around me.

"I toughed it out for four more months, when mercifully God intervened through the church's finance committee to end my nightmare. Even before I was hired, the church was deep in debt from a past building program. Money was tight, so the committee decided that something had to be done immediately to save the church some money. Since no one on the committee was sure what I was supposed to be doing in my ministry, the committee felt that the easiest way to save money was to eliminate my position. The church agreed.

"The day that the church voted on this action was the second-happiest day of my life, because I knew Charles couldn't abuse me anymore. God kept me out of full-time ministry for a couple of years to heal my wounds. I currently serve as pastor of a loving church and am once again excited about being in ministry.

"P.S. I know many other associate ministers who have gone through horrendous experiences like mine, and I trust your book will be a great encouragement to us all."

I have numerous stories like this in my files. They are very sad to read. Several commonalities permeate most of these pastor-staff conflicts.

Pastor-Staff Conflict

Most pastor-staff conflict situations have certain elements in common. The pastor's leadership style tends to be authoritarian rather than team oriented. An authoritarian pastor perceives himself as boss of the staff and gives orders that are never to be questioned. There is no room for any input from staff members. They are to do simply what they are told.

Job descriptions, if there are any, tend to be vague and overly general. This leaves staff ministers guessing what their responsibilities are or looking to the senior pastor to issue all of the directives of duty. When a staff minister is considering an associate position in a new church situation, a job description should be expected and meticulously examined. If a request for one is denied or left open-ended with an "Oh, we'll take care of that after you join the staff," this is a red flag, a warning not to accept such a position. Poorly written job descriptions need to be rewritten with clear and specific language. Don't accept a position until this matter is settled.

Staff ministers in conflicted situations usually did not do their homework before accepting the position. They did not check into the senior pastor's history of staff relations. They did not talk with former associates who had worked with him in the past. Pathological senior pastors nearly always leave a trail of pastor-staff conflicts, in either present or prior churches. Such pastors rarely change from cooperative, kind, responsible ministers with loving dispositions into harsh, demanding, authoritarian, impersonal monsters overnight.

Pastor-staff conflict situations often reveal that minor attention has been given to regular staff meetings where both short-range and long-range planning is emphasized and where everyone's responsibilities are clearly explained in the context of a team effort. Where there are few if any regular staff meetings, communication tends to be poor and major problems are more likely to arise. It is not uncommon to find conflicted staff situations where three to four months go by without a staff meeting. Authoritarian pastors will arbitrarily issue orders and plans by memorandum from the pastor's study to the various staff members. No consultations. No feedback. No questions. No staff input. Just do your job, whether you like it or not. No staff member will dare question the directives of such a pastor for fear of losing his job. By the way, with such a staff situation there will be few smiles or any wholesome laughter.

Where pastor-staff conflict prevails, there is usually a "hired-hand" attitude toward staff members. Such persons are hired as in secular business to do a certain job. There tends to be among pathological pastors and their lay leaders a lack of awareness of calling from God for staff associates. Of course, there is always a sense of calling for the senior pastor in such situations. He always has the blessing of God's call on him, but the other staff ministers are merely employees who may be hired and fired at will. This attitude may be observed among most of the lay leaders in a church where pastor-staff conflict prevails.

Causes of Conflict

Several specific causes of conflict between ministers of a staff may also be observed where pathological ministers are found. A personality clash is often reported by staff associates. Such a clash usually involves some type of relational competition rather than cooperation. One sees the other as some kind of threat. Pathological senior pastors tend to be very insecure and perceive a certain staff member as a threat to his status in the eyes of the congregation.

Personality clashes may also involve a clash in values or beliefs. Some pathological senior pastors are very often workaholics. If an associate tends to be laid back, easygoing, or unmotivated, such a pastor's work ethic (especially if connected with type A behavior) will strongly clash with his perceived "lazy" associate (who may express type B behavior).[1] Another basic difference of belief may be that the senior minister considers himself the boss, while his associate may believe that staff ministers ought to be team members, with the senior pastor being primus inter pares, the first among equals. Such differing beliefs can easily cause clashes.

Similarly, jealousy can be the cause of intrastaff conflict. Pathological senior pastors who are very insecure will feel threatened by an overly popular associate. If an associate's anniversaries or birthdays are given more attention by the congregation than those of the pastor, jealousy will set in and eventually erupt into conflict.

If a pastor lays unrealistic expectations on an associate, conflict is inevitable. Associate Pastor Tom is a typical example of this. His senior pastor was such a driven workaholic with a desperate need to succeed that he drove Tom beyond realistic expectations. When the pressure finally caused Tom to snap, then conflict was the result. No associate wants his pastor to constantly ride his back regarding the details of his work assignments. He simply wants to be trusted to perform within the limits of reason.

Poor communication within the staff can be another cause of conflict. It appears that many pathological ministers expect staff persons to be able to read their minds. It seems never to occur to them to communicate their instructions in clear and direct language. A church staff can become quickly confused if not paralyzed when there is poor communication coming from the top. One form of poor communication may be when a senior pastor sends mixed signals to his staff. One week he may issue instructions that for some unexplained reason he contradicts the next week. Pathological ministers can easily exhibit such indecision and then blame the confused staff when the results are not what he wants.

Philosophical differences may also cause conflict within a staff. Some pathological ministers believe the church was made for them and not that they were made for the church. Such persons perceive the entire church program as the means to advance their personal ambitions and careers. The associates of such pastors will soon begin to feel used and thus expendable. This is not a good work environment. The purpose of the church is to glorify God and not the pastor. But a pathological, arrogant pastor never gets that message.

Types of Abuse

A brief description of the various types of abuse that staff ministers may experience at the hands of pathological senior pastors could prove helpful to both ministers and lay leaders in preventing or correcting such abuses.

Slave-Driver Treatment

First, there is the slave-driver treatment described by Associate Pastor Tom. Pastor Charles saw Tom as a thing to be used for the senior pastor's own advancement, not as a person in his own right. Charles would never have tolerated his deacons treating him the way he treated Tom. Tom was only a means that would help Charles get what he wanted. Tom was a hired hand, a church slave to be expended for Charles's own ambitions. To push a person beyond his human limits is abusive treatment, pure and simple, especially when there is no appreciation for the hard work being done.

Silent Treatment

Several associate ministers have told me of working with a senior pastor who rarely speaks to them, even in the office during the week, who has no words of encouragement or public or private affirmation of any kind. One associate wrote, "Most of the time my pastor simply ignores me. I never know what he's thinking. I just assume that his silence is indicative of his disapproval over something I've done or not done. When I ask him if something is wrong, he replies, 'Oh, nothing; everything is fine.' But I know better. I'm left wondering. No one likes to work with a person like that."

Related to the silent treatment is the distance treatment. One associate minister told me he had worked with a senior pastor for more than five years and not once had he and his wife been invited to any kind of social gathering in the pastor's home. Not once had the pastor invited him to lunch. There was no friendship relationship between them. Working together in the same church in a variety of responsibilities, they might as well have been working a thousand miles apart. This associate concluded that his pastor simply did not like him. It made for a very lonely work situation, to say the least. In my judgment, this is a form of abuse. In family life, we call it neglect.

Public Criticism

In contrast to the silent treatment, there is public criticism in group gatherings. Verbal castigations before the congregation or in smaller groups can be very embarrassing, even humiliating, and thus abusive. One associate minister who was in charge of the church education program told of how his senior pastor would make snide remarks from the pulpit about why the Sunday school attendance was declining, such as, "Some of you have been asking why our Bible study program attendance is dropping off . . . well if our minister of education would spend as much time doing Sunday school work as he does reading his daily mail, we might see our attendance grow . . . ha, ha, ha." This wasn't funny and no one laughed but the pastor.

Another senior pastor would publicly blame his minister of education for things he had not done. For example, the senior pastor scheduled a church women's group and an evangelism meeting on the same day. When he realized the conflict, he publicly blamed the associate for it. This pastor refused to take responsibility for his own actions and often made his associate the fall guy. Obviously this associate lost respect for his pastor who not only shifted the blame but lied about it after the damage was done.

Constant Blame

There is the catch-22 treatment: The associate is condemned if he does and condemned if he doesn't—also called the no-win situation. This kind of treatment assures that regardless of what this staff member does or does not do, he will be blamed for any negative results. He becomes the scapegoat for whatever goes wrong in the church program.

Sudden Termination

Some associates have described their experience of being abused as the stab-in-the-back treatment. One staff minister told of being invited to join the staff of a man he had known for several years. "I thought we were good friends, although we had never worked together," he said. "But not long after I joined his staff, the relationship changed. I had no idea this pastor was so two-faced. He had lied to me about the situation in the church, saying everything was wonderful. I soon discovered that was not true. The finances were in bad shape, he was in conflict with the deacons, and there was a high turnover rate among the secretaries and other support personnel. Then one day, after I had been there only a few weeks, he called me into his office and said I would have to leave. When I asked why, he responded, 'Because you just aren't working out like we expected. Your job performance is unacceptable.' When I pressed for details, he refused any specifics. I was in shock. I felt stabbed in the back."

A very common use of the sudden-termination treatment is the practice of some senior pastors who, on arriving to take their new position, require some or all of the remaining staff persons to submit their resignations, allegedly to give the new minister the freedom to name his own staff personnel.

Sometimes this strategy is worked out by a prospective minister in advance with the pastor search committee, who make this a part of their recommendation of the new minister. In effect, this would mean saying to the church, "If you call this person as our minister, then you will be asking all of the staff persons to submit their resignations." Of course, it is usually explained that the new minister may request certain or even all of the existing staff persons to remain in place after his arrival, but the decision will be his. Naturally, this leaves subordinate staff persons in a very insecure position, since their future hinges on the choice of the incoming minister rather than on the will of the entire congregation, regardless of the acceptability of their previous work in this church. Any minister who would follow this procedure needs to think twice about requiring a long-term staff person, who is highly respected by the congregation, to resign. I have seen several instances where such action resulted in the minister himself having to leave before too long.

Sudden termination of a staff minister is sometimes demanded with no explanation whatsoever. It is a horrible experience for a staff minister to find himself being fired for no concrete reason. And it is even worse to be fired for reasons that have no substance to them or because of accusations that are simply not true. Similar to this is the termination that is contrived, executed behind one's back, and schemed by a senior pastor–dominated personnel committee. The staff minister comes to work one day and discovers a letter of dismissal on his desk from the personnel committee. He is to be out of his office by the end of the week; maybe his salary will be paid for two weeks if he is fortunate. A few personnel committees might offer a severance package of salary and benefits for one to three months. The implication of the letter is simply, "Don't give us any trouble over this; just be gone by the suggested date." Cruel? Believe me, it happens.

Some terminations are simply blunt, totally insensitive, without any regard for the person and that person's family. One day he is working diligently, happily, productively; then the next day he finds himself dismissed from his job with nowhere to go. One staff minister told me that one day his senior pastor and one of the deacons walked into his office and bluntly told him to clean out his desk, leave the building, and don't come back. When he asked why, what had he done or not done, the pastor responded, "I don't have to give you a reason; just go." To be sure, this rarely happens, but to those who have experienced this kind of treatment, it is a major blow that is extremely difficult to bear. Abuse is abuse however it happens.

Personality Disorders of Abusive Pastors

Why are some pastors so abusive to their staff members? Many if not most of these pastors are afflicted with one of the following personality disorders. The American Psychiatric Association publication DSM-IV lists ten specific personality disorders. It appears to me from my research that at least five of these are sometimes seen among ministers. A brief review of these five will suffice to reveal something of the problem churches face when their pastor is so afflicted.

The Paranoid Minister

First, there is the paranoid person, one who is suspicious and quick to take offense. Such a person has few confidants and may read hidden meaning into innocent remarks. The paranoid minister will have unfounded suspicion that another is deceiving, exploiting, or harming him. He will be preoccupied with unjustified doubts as to the loyalty or trustworthiness of associates or friends. He will be reluctant to confide in others, due to unwarranted fears that information will be maliciously used against him. There may be a perception of hidden, demeaning, or threatening content in ordinary events or comments and a persistent bearing of grudges. He may perceive personal attacks on his reputation or character that is not perceived by others; then this person responds quickly with anger or counterattacks. There could also be unjustified, recurring suspicions about the fidelity/loyalty of spouse or work associates. If at least four of the above traits are present in a variety of situations, then this person is a victim of paranoid personality disorder.[2]

Borderline Personality Disorder

There is considerable debate as to who actually belongs in the category of borderline personality disorder. To be sure, these are generally very sick people, but it appears to me that some abusive pastors are afflicted with this condition. These persons sustain a pattern of instability throughout their adult lives, appearing often to be in a crisis of mood, behavior, or interpersonal relationships. Many feel empty and bored; they may attach themselves strongly to others, then become intensely angry or hostile when they believe that they are being ignored or mistreated by those they depend on. Some may even try to harm themselves in anger and desperation (up to 10 percent commit suicide). They are in deep emotional pain. Intense and rapid mood swings, impulsivity, and unstable interpersonal relationships make it difficult for them to achieve their full potential socially, at work, or at home. Anger is a very serious problem for them, often out-of-control, inappropriate, and intense (demonstrated by frequent temper displays and a constant feeling of hostility). They cannot handle stress at all. Abusive pastors may not fully express this disorder, but they may approximate it to some degree.[3]

The Histrionic Minister

As with borderline personality disorder, an abusive pastor may not be fully expressive of the histrionic personality disorder, but he may approximate it. Overly emotional, vague, and attention-seeking, histrionic people need constant reassurance that they are attractive. The typical victim is female, but the disorder can occur in males. The following traits may be observed: discomfort with situations in which the person is not the center of attention; relationships that are frequently fraught with inappropriately seductive or sexually provocative behavior; expression of emotion that is shallow and rapidly shifting; frequent focusing of attention on self through use of physical appearance; speech that is vague; overly dramatic expression of emotion; easy suggestibility, being readily influenced by opinions of other people or by circumstances; belief that relationships are more intimate than they really are. If five of the above traits are observed in someone, that person is considered histrionic.[4] Several of the pastors described in my correspondence with abused staff ministers easily fit into this category.

The Narcissistic Minister

Beginning early in adult life, the person with narcissistic personality disorder has a lifelong pattern of grandiosity (fantasized or actual), lack of empathy, and need for admiration, which is present in a variety of situations and shown by at least five of the following: a grandiose sense of self-importance (the person exaggerates his own abilities and accomplishments); preoccupation with fantasies of beauty, brilliance, ideal love, power, or limitless success; belief that personal uniqueness renders the person fit only for association with (or understanding by) people or institutions of rarefied status; need for excessive admiration; a sense of entitlement (the person unreasonably expects favorable treatment or automatic granting of his wishes); exploitation of others to achieve personal goals; lack of empathy; frequent envy of others or belief that others envy him; and arrogance or haughtiness in attitude or behavior.[5]

A disturbingly high percentage of pathological pastors referred to and described in the correspondence of my research clearly fit into the narcissistic category. For obvious reasons, the ministry seems to attract such persons. They tend to be very insecure and ignored people who believe that the ministry will give them the security and attention they have not found elsewhere. Some were raised in a family that conveyed to them a "child-of-destiny" syndrome. The ministry offers to them the means whereby they will become the person of significance that their home taught them they were. But, unfortunately, they were not taught the mitigating virtues of humility, compassion, unselfishness, and respect for others needed to give a Christian balance to their sense of significance.

The Obsessive-Compulsive Minister

Beginning by early adult life, the obsessive-compulsive personality is preoccupied with control, orderliness, and perfection more than with efficiency, flexibility, and candor. These behaviors are present in a variety of situations, including at least four of the following: absorption with details, lists, order, organization, rules, or schedules to such an extent that the purpose of the activity is lost; perfectionistic to a degree that interferes with completing the task; workaholic (works to the exclusion of leisure activities); overly conscientious, inflexible, or scrupulous about ethics, morals, or values to a degree out of keeping with cultural or religious influence; attached to worthless items of no real or sentimental value; uncooperative or unwilling to delegate tasks unless others agree to do things this person's way; stingy, hoarding money against future need; and rigid and stubborn. Moreover, this person resists the authority of others but insists on his own. The obsessive-compulsive disorder is fairly common and is found more often in males than in females. It probably runs in families.[6]

The ministry naturally puts a lot of pressure on ministers to be perfect in order to claim to be the servant of a perfect God. This pressure can easily get out of control and become a personality disorder. Perfectionistic pastors are extremely difficult to work with because they naturally expect perfection from their associates, since the work of their associates reflects back on the pastor-supervisor. Pastors need to follow the "laid-back Jesus" who, though perfect, was flexible and not perfectionistic. Perfectionistic pastors become harsh taskmasters who drive their associates to despair.

Brain Damage

Finally, there is a category not discussed in the personality disorder section of the DSM-IV. I have known some pathological pastors whose behavior appears to be due to some type of brain damage. Through the years I have observed certain pastors who suffered head injuries in an automobile accident. These men, prior to their accidents, were congenial, cooperative, and normal persons in every aspect of their behavior. But following a severe head injury and recovery, their personality appeared radically altered. Each one began to exhibit aggressive, accusatory behavior toward staff associates and various lay leaders, untypical of their past behavior toward these same persons. This is not intended to be a medical explanation but simply an observation that heretofore normal people sometimes become difficult to work with following a traumatic head injury or brain surgery.

Associate Pastor Gerry described his experience: "One summer my senior pastor had brain surgery for a blood clot, after which his behavior radically changed. Within a short time, he began to take away my responsibilities and became openly hostile toward me. When I asked to discuss the problem, I was told by the pastor to meet with him and the personnel committee chairman the next morning. In that meeting the senior pastor degraded and berated me for over an hour (all feelings, no facts). The pastor spoke like a crazy man, there being no dialogue, and when he was finished, he walked out of the room. I did not realize that this was my yearly evaluation. The pastor scored me a 3 out of 10, while I had scored 10 each of the two previous years.

"I immediately began sending out my résumé, hoping to give the Lord opportunity to open doors. I begged the pastor to wait on the Lord with me, but he just wanted me gone. Over the next few weeks, my wife and I suffered much abuse and hatefulness, so we finally chose to resign with nowhere to go. It was financially devastating and emotionally traumatic. But the Lord finally delivered me, and I was called to another church."

Gerry's wife commented, "Being forced to leave your home and friends when you've done nothing wrong is AWFUL! But, as in all things, God's grace was more than sufficient and wonderfully abundant."

Gerry is now serving in a very fine church as an associate to a very fine pastor in a challenging and growing church. Looking back, Gerry says he can date the change in the senior pastor from the time of his brain surgery. Incidentally, that particular pastor went on to an even larger church but didn't last more than a few months due to his erratic behavior. Today he is no longer in the ministry.

Wayne Oates has dealt with these disorders in his seminal book *Behind the Masks,* saying:

> What gets us . . . is finding these disorders of everyday life in the conduct of fellow church members. We are alternately alarmed or sweet-talked and enchanted by them if they are pastors, ministers of music, ministers of education, ministers of youth, or prominent lay leaders in the church. In these instances, such persons' outlandish behaviors become the topic of many telephone conversations between church members. They are the favorite subject of rumors generated in the imaginations of people who otherwise would have little to talk about and even less to think about. In this sense, persons with such ways of life thrive on the boredom of other people. . . . These ordinarily are sane people, but they wear their sanity as a mask, not as the outward expression of an inward possession. They are religious, but we are mystified that neither the sacraments of the liturgical churches nor the ordinances and 'professions of faith' of the churches of the revival traditions have changed their obstinate ways of life, but have only glossed them over with a veneer of religiosity.[7]

Protecting the Abused Staff Minister

So how can churches protect the abused staff minister from pathological senior pastors? I recommend three strategies: first, structured protection; second, self-protection; and third, specific steps in prevention.

Structured Protection

Here is an opportunity for the ministers' advisory council to function on behalf of all staff ministers. I will explain the role of this council more fully in the next chapter, but I just want to say here that this group of carefully selected people can serve as a court of appeal whenever a pathological minister launches an unwarranted attack on a staff minister. If a senior pastor suddenly tells a staff minister to turn in his resignation, the staff person can take the matter directly to the ministers' advisory council. The council can then weigh the pastor's accusations against the staff minister's responses. If other testimony is needed, they can ask for it. The council will have the authority to make a final decision as to the staff minister's future. They may serve as a reconciliation group between the pastor and staff minister.

If the senior pastor is truly pathological and thus unreasonable and emotionally unstable, the council will need to deal with the pastor's larger problem, which is himself. If the problem is only misinformation or a misunderstanding, the council can help to resolve the problem and get the two pastors back to working harmoniously together. The council will want to get a job evaluation report from the personnel committee that covers at least the past two years of the associate pastor's service. If the problem is a pathological pastor, then the council needs to protect the unfairly accused staff minister and seek to get help for the senior pastor's emotional problems.

Self-Protection

Where there is no ministers' advisory council, a staff minister may want to consult with the chairperson of the personnel committee regarding difficulties with the senior minister. Hopefully, personnel committee guidelines will offer direction. Moreover, a staff minister is advised to keep a file documenting problematic incidents with the senior minister (include witnesses) for later referral if called to account. In addition, an attitude of kindness, cooperation, and respect will always strengthen a staff minister's position.

Prevention

There are some specific steps in the area of prevention that will go a long way toward protecting staff ministers from troubled, authoritarian senior pastors. The ministers' advisory council could establish guidelines that would prohibit the arbitrary termination of staff ministers on the arrival of a new pastor. The church's pastor search committee would know this and so inform any new pastor being recommended to the church.

In addition, it is always helpful, even necessary for good work, for specific job descriptions to be outlined by the personnel committee whenever a new staff minister is brought in. It is unrealistic, unfair, and arbitrary for a staff minister to be told that his job is "to do whatever the pastor wants you to do." A new staff minister needs to be instructed specifically as to what will be expected of him. Along with this, an annual evaluation by the personnel committee will give the staff minister a picture of how well the job description is being followed.

Moreover, the church needs to establish a clear chain of command regarding staff ministers. Who is responsible to whom? In most churches, it seems that the senior pastor is best suited to be the supervisor of the entire staff. The personnel committee functions to see to it that this supervision is handled smoothly in the context of a team approach. If a clear job description is in place, a staff minister should never be insubordinate to the pastor and do whatever he pleases. If a pastor is unfair and heavy-handed, then the staff minister can ask for a hearing from the ministers' advisory council. The council needs to work closely with and in cooperation with the personnel committee to resolve these difficulties, but the council is the last court of appeal for each staff person, including the pastor. The personnel committee sets the standards for employment, develops the job descriptions, evaluates the work of staff members, and recommends employment of staff to the church. But the council is the final court for resolving problems among staff. They are there to protect and encourage all staff persons.

Finally, it is very important for a church to establish a philosophy of teamwork among all staff ministers. Both the personnel committee and the ministers' advisory council should work to accomplish this. In the early church it appears that pastors were considered the first among equals. This is still a sound principle for staffs today. If a minister reveals himself to be pathological, authoritarian, or emotionally unstable, thus making teamwork impossible, the ministers' advisory council must step in and deal with this problem, difficult as it may be. No church can afford to stand by and allow a staff minister to be abused by leadership.

A church must protect its staff ministers at all costs. When churches allow their ministers to be abused, whether by pathological lay leaders or pastors, they will pay a very high price for a very long time.

part 3

Recovery and Healing

11 A Ministers' Advisory Council

The New Testament is clear that the apostles were not intimidated by moral and organizational threats to the welfare of the church. They knew that evil in the church had to be dealt with quickly and thoroughly. And we must follow their lead. The church must rid itself of clergy killers and pathological antagonists. Sometimes even excommunication is necessary.

Some Biblical Precedents

Paul urged the church at Corinth to expel one of its members who was living immorally with his stepmother (1 Cor. 5:1–8). As we have seen, he also called on that same church to negate the influence of certain "super-apostles" (2 Cor. 11:5; 12:11), "false apostles" (2 Cor. 11:13), and "deceitful workers, disguising themselves as apostles of Christ" (2 Cor. 11:13). He identified them with Satan (2 Cor. 11:14).

The apostle John felt strongly about the evil influence of one church leader named Diotrephes:

I have written something to the church; but Diotrephes, who likes to put himself first, does not acknowledge our authority. So if I come, I will call attention to what he is doing in spreading false charges against us. And not content with those charges, he refuses to welcome the friends, and even prevents those who want to do so and expels them from the church.

> Beloved, do not imitate what is evil but imitate what is good. Whoever does good is from God; whoever does evil has not seen God.
>
> 3 John 9–11

Even though John does not directly urge that Diotrephes be excommunicated from the church, he leaves no doubt about the evil influence of this man. It would be surprising, however, if this church, after reading John's evaluation of Diotrephes, continued to tolerate his presence in the fellowship.

Paul's language to the church at Corinth regarding the immoral member living with his stepmother is quite clear: He is to be "removed" from among the congregation (1 Cor. 5:2) and handed over "to Satan for the destruction of the flesh, so that his spirit may be saved in the day of the Lord" (1 Cor. 5:5).

Concerning the antagonistic Judaizers who hounded Paul's ministry at Corinth and tried to discredit his apostolic authority, a reading of 2 Corinthians 10–13 reveals a very stern rebuke of those who would undercut his leadership. He concludes by threatening to be severe with the church when he returns to Corinth if this problem is not corrected (2 Cor. 13:10), and he urges the church, "Put things in order, listen to my appeal, agree with one another, live in peace; and the God of love and peace will be with you" (2 Cor. 13:11).

Where did the apostles learn to teach the churches to beware of evil leaders? Jesus himself had taught this. He urged them to beware of the "yeast [teaching] of the Pharisees and Sadducees" (Matt. 16:6, 12), some of whom were evil leaders in Israel. In addition, the apostles could never forget Jesus' warning:

> Beware of the scribes, who like to walk around in long robes, and to be greeted with respect in the marketplaces, and to have the best seats in the synagogues and places of honor at banquets! They devour widows' houses and for the sake of appearance say long prayers. They will receive the greater condemnation.
>
> Mark 12:38–40

These descriptive words remind me of the pathological antagonists and clergy killers who do great harm to ministers of the gospel.

170

The nature of opposition to God's servants hasn't changed much in two thousand years.

A Strategy of Protection

How are these types of people to be dealt with in the church today? Several ideas will be suggested here, their foundation being the ministers' advisory council. Not all of these ideas will work in every church. Each church must design its own bulwark to protect its ministers from abusers, but the following may stimulate even better ideas. The idea of a ministers' advisory council was suggested earlier in chapters 5 and 10, but here I will go into greater detail regarding its establishment and function.

Determining a strategy to protect its ministers is the responsibility of the entire church congregation, but the details must be worked out by a smaller group, some type of ad hoc committee elected by the church. This workable strategy should not be devised by the official board, especially if the problem of antagonism is located primarily therein. This would simply give any antagonists on the board more power to oppose the pastor.

This ad hoc committee should be made up of both men and women, young and old, single and married, being truly representative of the congregation. The group should have no more than ten members. A standing nominating committee could bring to the church a recommended list of names, or they could be nominated from the floor of the church in business session by asking everyone to propose a list of ten names (if that is the desired number). Those getting the most nominations would make up the committee, and the one with the most nominations would be the chairperson.

I suggest that the ad hoc committee develop the idea of a ministers' advisory council and recommend this strategy to the church. The ad hoc committee would recommend that a ministers' advisory council be elected by the church and be as representative of the congregation as possible, similar to the representativeness of the ad hoc committee itself. Its size should be no larger than twelve. Beyond that number a group becomes unwieldy. The chairperson (either male or female) should be someone who has the highest respect of the congregation and who has a proven record of being a loving supporter of the church's ministers. All staff ministers of the church would join in this council's meetings, possibly as ex-officio members.

Under no circumstances should any person who has a reputation of being an antagonist or troublemaker be placed on the council. To put such a person there would be like putting a fox in the henhouse. Every member of the council must be a mature and deeply devoted Christian, someone who can be loving, honest, and firm in dealing with problems in the congregation. These persons must not be easily influenced or intimidated by people of perceived power, whether ministers or nonministers. From the judgment of my experience as a pastor, I would recommend that the pastor or senior minister be asked to approve any final list of members before it is presented to the church. Council members need to be the minister's friends, not his enemies. Antagonists are usually smart enough to get themselves nominated to such a powerful group, and the pastor or senior minister should have veto power to keep such persons off the council.

The members of the council would serve three-year terms, with the first council being divided into three groups of those serving a one-year term, a two-year term, and a three-year term. The standing nominating committee of the church would recommend the new members each year.

The council would carry the full authority of the church and would be independent and free of influence of any other group in the church, including the official board (deacons, elders, and others). The council would meet once per quarter or as often as needed. A time of congregational crisis might require meeting once a week until the crisis passes. Their meetings would be confidential, not reporting to the church unless necessary.

A document describing the nature, organization, and functions of the council should be incorporated into the church bylaws. This could have a restraining influence on any potential antagonist in the church.

The Mission and Function of the Council

The mission of the ministers' advisory council is to serve as a group of encouragers for all the ministers on the church staff; to serve as a buffer from any attacks on the church's ministers from any source either within or without the congregation; to give advice and suggestions to the church's ministers regarding their work; to hear and resolve complaints from anyone in the congregation or from the ministers themselves regarding any topic that relates to the welfare of the church; to resolve differences among the church staff ministers; and, if necessary, to recommend that the church excommunicate any member who stubbornly persists in antagonizing any of the ministers of the church.

Obviously there are a variety of ways that the above mission of the council could be carried out. The following is suggestive as to how it might function.

Encouragement

The council would serve primarily as encouragers of the ministerial staff. Ministers are human and need to be complimented when they are doing a good job. Each meeting of the council should begin with words of praise and affirmation of these servants of the Lord. The council could also take the initiative to affirm the ministers in public by means of a special ministers' appreciation Sunday or banquet and special anniversary recognitions each year with gifts of appreciation, including gifts to the ministers' families (see 1 Tim. 5:17–18). The latter would include recommendations to the personnel committee regarding Christmas bonuses rather than leaving such a decision to a lone church treasurer, as is done in some churches. My survey of church antagonists reveals that the church treasurer is often an antagonist who volunteers for the treasurer's job as a self-appointed watchdog of the church treasury.

Protection

The council would serve as a buffer against any attacks from antagonists. The church's personnel policies should include a stipulation that any complaint against a minister of the church must be brought before the council in person by the one(s) making the accusation or it will not be considered a valid complaint. There must be two or more witnesses (see Deut. 19:1–21 and 1 Tim. 5:19) regarding any accusation against a minister. If the accusers are not willing to follow these requirements, the church should be told to ignore and disregard the accusations of these people, and the accusers should be disciplined accordingly by being told either to desist from their criticisms or to leave the church. (See disciplinary function below.)

Advisory

The council would serve as a support group of reputable and trustworthy church members to offer advice on those topics related to the ministers' responsibilities—those duties spelled out in the job descriptions of the ministerial staff. In the assured confidentiality of private council meetings, council members should feel free to bring up such matters as length of sermons, sermon topics, and the manner of delivery of sermons; the details of the order of worship services; the ministers' demeanor at funerals, weddings, and counseling; and the ministers' visitation program. Other concerns that might come up could include the ministers' manner of dealing with people in either individual or group settings and his relationship with the other staff ministers and office secretaries. The goal would be to improve relationships and performance. This would not imply that this council could usurp the role of an elected personnel committee but would serve only in an advisory capacity regarding personnel relationships.

Some churches provide suggestion boxes in high-traffic areas of the church facilities where members can place written suggestions, either positive or negative. This council could be in charge of these boxes or serve as a "living suggestion box" to whom members could express their ideas. Such suggestions could then be shared with the ministers.

Resolution

The council would serve as a problem-solving group regarding any unresolved problems that exist between any church member and any staff minister, following the above requirements for those making accusations. As an example, a church treasurer refuses to approve any requisitions of funds from the youth minister. Requisitions from the music minister are readily approved but not for the youth minister, since the treasurer has no personal interest in the youth program. Both the senior pastor and finance committee chairperson refuse to deal with the problem. The youth minister can then take this problem to the council for resolution.

Reconciliation

The council would serve as an agent of reconciliation between offended/offending parties in the congregation when one or more of the staff ministers are involved. This might include a staff conflict between two persons that is beyond the guidelines of the church personnel committee. As an example, a church treasurer accuses the youth minister of using the church phone for personal long-distance calls. The treasurer makes this untrue accusation before several groups when the youth minister is not there to defend himself. The council handles such false accusations by calling the treasurer before them and demanding proof of his accusations. If proof is not forthcoming, the council requires either a public apology or resignation of the treasurer.

Discipline

The council would serve with the authority of the church to deal in a disciplinary manner with any antagonistic person who consistently harasses a minister of the church. The council would have the authority of the church to call such a person before the council to discuss his or her antagonistic actions. If this person refuses to stop the harassment of the minister, this person would be asked to leave the church. If this person refuses to leave, then the council will take the matter to the congregation with the recommendation that this person be excommunicated from the fellowship. As one layman once told his pastor when this type of problem was being discussed, "Pastor, sometimes the only way to deal with a boil is to lance it to drain the poison." Referring to the treasurer of the church, the layman continued, "He is a boil on our church." However, at that time, there was no mechanism in the organizational life of the church such as a ministers' advisory council with power to deal with toxic antagonists.

The Intentional Protection of Ministers from Attack

The ministers' advisory council is certainly no cure-all, but it is a step in the right direction to provide intentional protection of the church's ministers from attack by pathological antagonists and clergy killers. It is imperative that a church realize that such threats to its ministers are always a possibility. It is best to be prepared for such perils in advance rather than waiting for a crisis to become full-blown.

When an antagonist joins a church usually no one has any idea that he will become a major problem. Few church members have the theological or psychological insight necessary to perceive a shallow-thinking person with deep-rooted spiritual problems and psychological instability. Even when a person's life has been characterized by long-standing anger issues and his behavior has revealed contradictory moral standards, no one can know that he is a church time bomb just waiting to go off. Manipulators are often quite charming.

It is crucial that a church plan in advance for the intentional protection of its ministers from attack. It is my judgment that one of the best ways to do this is through the ministers' advisory council.

Relation of the Council to the Personnel Committee

Most churches have a personnel committee. What would be the relation of this committee to the ministers' advisory council? The personnel committee covers a broad area of responsibility by establishing personnel policies for *all* employees, including job descriptions that are spelled out in a personnel handbook and approved by the church. With these guidelines, the committee gives regular supervision to all employees, including ministerial staff, receptionists, secretaries, custodians, kitchen and nursery helpers who are paid, bookkeepers, and so on, as per their published job descriptions. The committee would recommend annual salary and benefit packages to the finance or budget committee and resolve any complaints regarding nonministerial staff.[1]

The personnel committee serves as an employment committee for any nonministerial staff position. A special ad hoc search committee is usually elected by the church to secure persons for any of the ministerial staff positions, including that of senior pastor. In some cases, however, the ministers' advisory council could serve as an ad hoc search committee for filling ministerial positions.

The ministers' advisory council would be exclusively responsible for the ministerial staff in the areas of encouragement, protection, advice, resolution of any intrastaff problems or complaints from church members, reconciliation between offended/offending parties in the congregation when any staff minister is involved, recognizing that the council has the authority to recommend to the church disciplinary action for anyone who is disrupting the unity and fellowship of the church, after all other avenues of resolution have been unsuccessfully followed.

The chairpersons of these two groups (the ministers' advisory council and the personnel committee) would need to work very closely with the pastor to maintain maximum cooperation and respect for each other's delegated duties. Each church will need to devise a plan best suited for its needs to assist its ministerial staff and support personnel.

12 Steps toward Healing for Abused Clergy

The wounded minister will always be a minister at heart, so his first concern while struggling with woundedness should not be self-pity, anger, or revenge, but healing. Otherwise the abusers win. If healing does not take place, the effect of the abuse will flow over like a poison into other facets of a wounded minister's life and work. The unhealed wounded minister will have either a toxic ministry or no ministry at all. Surely a sincere minister does not want that. So how does a wounded minister move toward healing? There are several steps to take.

Face the Consequences of Abuse

It seems to me that the first step toward healing is for the wounded minister to face realistically the consequences of having been abused in the process of ministry in a church. In any hospital emergency room a good doctor will take a close look at a new patient's wounds before deciding what to do. It is no different with the healing of a wounded minister.

Feeling Betrayed

A wounded minister has been deeply hurt, but what is the nature of that hurt? First, he feels betrayed by those who once pledged to support him in his ministry. I once asked one of my detractors if he had voted in the affirmative when the church called me as the pastor. He replied that he had. I said that such a vote was also a vote to support me and not sit back and criticize me. He thought for a moment and then said, "Well, I never thought of it like that." Then I said, "Well, think about it now." Shortly thereafter he and his wife left the church. It seems never to occur to such people that voting to call a minister is a vote to get behind him and follow his leadership, supporting him in every way possible.

Anger

The hurt the abused minister feels is often veiled anger. Why do some people want to hurt their minister? Do they get some pleasure from it? Are they religious sadists? Antagonists rarely if ever apologize for their injurious behavior. They seem to see no wrong in causing havoc in the church. Their incessant criticisms do irreparable damage to the life and witness of the church, which invariably reflects back on the minister. For this they show no remorse. Actually, they believe they are doing God a favor. With such people in the ranks of the church's leadership, no wonder a minister becomes so angry. But since there is an American cultural axiom that says, "It is not nice for a minister to show anger," he covers it up with deep hurt.

If the hurt is veiled anger, such anger is often deflected onto other people in rather subtle ways—arguments with his spouse and children, an angry tone of voice in his sermons, sharp comments made to other ministers and staff personnel.

Sometimes this veiled anger is turned inward toward himself, resulting in overeating, clinical depression, sleeplessness, drug abuse (smoking and drinking are two of the most common among depressed ministers), road rage, and so on. Anger turned inward, especially if long-term and persistent, can set a person up for a lot of medical problems as well.

Psychiatrist Leo Madow, in discussing how anger can hurt us, wrote:

> Anger can affect us adversely both physically and mentally. If we
> think of it as a form of energy which if repressed must come out

somewhere, we must recognize that it can harm almost any part of our body or influence our emotions and eventually our minds if a sufficient amount is accumulated.[1]

Dr. Madow then discusses some of the harmful results of anger—headaches, gastrointestinal disorders, respiratory disorders, skin disorders, genito-urinary disorders, arthritis, disabilities of the nervous system, and circulatory disorders. Among these problems he includes the ultimate harm—suicide.

There is now also strong evidence that long-term, persistent anger will eventually weaken the immune system of the body, making us vulnerable to such illnesses as cancer, heart trouble (especially that caused by the development of arteriosclerosis), and related medical problems.[2] Psychiatrist Redford Williams, and his historian wife, Virginia Williams, of Duke University have thoroughly documented these dangers.[3]

Loneliness

The hurt of a wounded minister involves the injury of extreme social and emotional loneliness and a feeling of abandonment. There is the perception that "no one really understands how I feel," sometimes including even the minister's spouse.[4] Several wounded ministers have told me that even when they turned to the available denominational leaders in their district or state, they met with little or no help. One told me, "These people responded in subtle ways but they did not want to really get involved." Another was told, "This is your problem, not mine." Baptist ministers are especially vulnerable because of the Baptist polity of local church autonomy. Denominational executives are extremely sensitive to the criticism of interfering with local church governance. Independent, nondenominational ministers have absolutely no outside church structure to come to their rescue.

In my own case, the top denominational executive made no effort to intervene, give supportive advice, or help me to relocate. As long as things were going well at the church and relationships seemed congenial, he was a very good friend to me in many ways, but when the antagonists began to attack me, he distanced himself. On the other hand, a denominational representative came, at my invitation, to a hostile deacons' meeting simply to observe, after which he commented, "They (the antagonists) are really an angry bunch of fellows." But he felt helpless to do anything about it.

Loneliness, therefore, is a major part of the injury of being abused. Those from whom you would appreciate assistance tend to stay away, never call, and leave you to yourself; no, they leave you to the wolves! Cowboys tell me it is a very lonely experience to be surrounded by a pack of wolves when you don't even have a gun to defend yourself.

These are only some of the consequences of the abuse experienced by wounded ministers, but they are probably the most serious ones. Other possible consequences are bitterness, cynicism (i.e., being contemptuously distrustful of human nature and motives), hopelessness, vengefulness or vindictiveness, self-pity, and depression (mentioned above as a result of anger turned inward). So facing these consequences as a form of diagnosis is the first step in the healing of abused clergy.

Find Competent Professional Counseling

An abused clergyperson must never try to deal with his injuries alone anymore than he would try to set his own broken leg. Clergy woundedness, inflicted by pathological antagonists or even well-intentioned dragons, must be seen as serious and in need of professional help. Therefore, a wounded minister will wisely seek competent and spiritually sensitive professional counseling.

There are many such therapists in practice today. Look in the yellow pages of your local telephone book under psychotherapists, clinical psychologists, or marriage and family counselors for those affiliated with such national organizations as the American Association of Pastoral Counselors (AAPC) or the American Association of Christian Counselors (AACC). However, even with such listings one must be careful, maybe even by trial and error, to locate the right therapist. You could also contact the national offices of these associations: American Association of Pastoral Counselors, 9504A Lee Highway, Fairfax, VA 22031-2303; 703-385-6967; e-mail: info@aapc.org; web site: http://www.aapc.org. American Association of Christian Counselors, P.O. Box 739, Forest, VA

24551-9973; 804-384-0564; web site: http://www.AACC.net. These sources can provide names, addresses, and phone numbers of members nearest you. Check the professional credentials of any of their referrals. The AACC is not an accrediting agency.

Another possible source for referral information would be to contact the departments of pastoral care or psychology and counseling of accredited theological seminaries in your region. These professors may be able to suggest competent Christian counselors close to you.

Some denominations provide well-trained counselors specifically for ministers in need of therapy and emotional support. Contact your regional or state denominational executive office for referral information. Such contacts are usually kept confidential and would not get back to your church or ministerial peers. These counseling offices are usually located somewhere other than the denominational offices for absolute privacy.

A few Christian therapists make their services available, especially to ministers, in retreat settings in one- or two-week periods of time.[5] Although these experiences are usually expensive, some medical insurance policies will cover part or most of the expense, especially if you get a referral by your personal physician or psychiatrist.

When you seek professional counseling, you may need to take along your spouse as well, and in some cases your family. As we have seen, for every wounded minister, there will be one or more members of his family who are hurting also for the same reasons. When antagonists attack a minister and try to terminate his position with the church, they almost never seem to care that they are also causing pain in the minister's spouse and children. One minister told me that when he confronted his major antagonist with the fact that his vicious criticisms were causing extreme nervous distress to his wife and teenage children, he replied, "Well, it's their tough luck that you are their husband and father."

The wounded minister, then, must not overlook his wounded family. They too may need professional counseling help.

Join a Ministers' Support Group

During the last half of the twentieth century, support groups of every sort began to emerge all over North America. These groups usually target specific needs: alcoholism, drug abuse, weight loss, divorce recovery, mental illness, cancer recovery, heart problems, singleness. Generally, they have proved to be very helpful. Wounded ministers will also benefit from a support group of their peers.

Wounded ministers, however, are hesitant to be involved in such a group and, even if they are willing, there may be no support group in their town or area (see chapter 14 on organizing a support group). A minister's natural hesitancy is related to the fear of exposure to his peers that he is in trouble. Related to this is the fear that the peers in the denomination will find out that he is not the super minister he wants them to think he is. One wounded pastor told me that when his peers and some of his denominational representatives found out he was in trouble, they began to distance themselves from him. They treated him like an outcast. He also discovered that some executives in high places in the denomination, in addition to some fellow ministers, would not recommend him to another church position.

In my humble judgment, a ministry peer support group is essential in the life of clergy today. Every minister, whether abused by his congregation or not, needs the insights, encouragement, and understanding of peers who are experiencing very similar challenges. No pastor should be without a peer support group. Wounded ministers especially need one.[6]

Learn to Deal Constructively with Anger

Nearly every wounded minister has a reservoir of long-standing and unhealthy anger. Anger is a normal, natural, and inevitable human emotion. It has certain positive functions—to correct injustice, protect from perceived threat, change unhealthy or undesirable circumstances. But anger, if long-term and persistent, can be unhealthy and damaging to one's physical, emotional, and relational welfare. Since most wounded ministers feel unfairly and unjustly treated, they are going to have to deal with their anger, hopefully constructively. How can this be done?

There are three basic ways people deal with anger. Some choose to vent their anger: yelling, screaming, throwing things, "blowing their top," throwing verbal temper tantrums, even breaking up the place. This is not wise. Someone is going to get hurt. People will certainly avoid a person who displays anger in this way. Venting one's anger also tends to make it worse. This kind of ventilation is psychologically unhealthy.

Others choose to repress their anger: shoving it down inside, covering it up, denying it, pulling back and pouting. Repressing anger in any way is an excellent recipe for depression, which is anger turned inward. This is also unhealthy, even dangerous. As we saw earlier in this chapter, repression of anger will break down the immune system of the body, making the person vulnerable to all kinds of physical and medical problems. Repression that leads to depression may also bring about thoughts of self-destruction. I have known some clinically depressed wounded ministers who eventually committed suicide.

The best way to deal constructively with anger is to learn how to talk about it. Express your feelings to a confidant who understands the stresses of the ministry. Use "I messages" rather than "you messages," addressing the problem or behavior rather than the person or persons involved. For example, "It makes me very angry when I am criticized behind my back with accusations that are unfair or untrue." Another example: "It angers me when anonymous letters are written to me containing lies or half-truths by sources that do not have all of the necessary facts." Also, "I get very angry when I come to a deacons' meeting and discover that a small group there is working from a hidden agenda that involves an attempt to pressure me into resigning for reasons that are not substantial or justifiable."

The confidant may be your spouse, a professional counselor, or a small group of supporters. If the church has established a ministers' advisory council, such a group could serve as a sounding board for your anger. Be careful, though, to use "I messages" and not to attack anyone directly by name. Such countercriticisms have a way of coming back to hurt a minister.

The following suggestions have proved helpful to many who seek to deal with anger constructively:

Seven Steps to Healthy Anger Release

1. *Recognize the anger you're feeling.* We may deny that we're angry because we feel too guilty about it. Denial turns the feeling inside where it seethes.

2. *Decide what made you angry.* Ask yourself the very important question: Is this worth getting angry over? If you can't forget it, then perhaps the source of your anger goes beyond a single event. Filter out the underlying cause of your grievance.

3. *Give the "provoker" the benefit of the doubt.* Instead of inflaming your anger by feeding yourself such reflections as, *Who does he think he is for treating me in this underhanded way!* suggest to yourself that perhaps this person is having a bad day or didn't intend to come across as he did.

4. *Count to ten and cool off.* Or practice some form of mental relaxation. There's nothing to be gained by an explosive outburst aimed at retaliation. Calm down first.

5. *Make your grievance known without attacking the other person.* This calls for tact and good communication skills. One important suggestion: Register your complaint using "I messages" instead of "you messages." For example, instead of saying, "*You're* acting unfairly and *you're* wrong," it's far more effective to say, "*I* feel hurt by what is happening."

6. *Listen.* Listen hard and try to understand. This is the key step in resolving the conflict and diffusing your anger.

7. *Forgive.* When we forgive someone, many positive psychological and physiological changes take place. We feel warm and more relaxed; we breathe more easily; we feel calmer; our blood pressure and heart rate drop; we may even cry tears of relief. But most important, through forgiveness we once again experience love, the highest essence of a relationship. We remember that we *care* about the other person. Is this why their behavior hurt us so much in the first place?[7]

Learn the Art of Forgiveness

One important goal or function of anger is to make a grievance known, but once that has been done, the offended must go *beyond* anger to forgiveness or else the anger tends to recur and do additional damage. Yet the main problem here is *how* to forgive. Yes, even ministers must learn how to forgive. As Lewis B. Smedes suggests, there is an art to forgiveness.[8] Learning the art of forgiveness is the best way to deal constructively with anger.

Forgiveness may not come easily for wounded ministers who may be holding onto a degree of self-righteousness. After all, are we not "servants of God"? So when we are attacked unjustly, it is only natural to desire justice rather than to forgive. B. H. Childs has defined *forgiveness* as "the act of rendering null and void the penalty owed by a wrongdoer to an offended party; hence a term having legal or quasi-legal qualities denoting a release from a debt."[9]

Steps in Forgiveness

According to Lewis Smedes, there are several steps in learning and practicing the art of forgiveness. I am still trying to learn and practice this art. It has been more than six years since Jack, the mean-spirited church officer of my last pastorate, caused me so much heartache and emotional pain. So as I try to explain Smedes's recommendations, I am writing out of my own struggles to forgive a person who did me so much harm.

Smedes says we must pass through three stages of forgiving.[10] First, we must rediscover the humanity of the person who hurt us. I have had to stop demonizing Jack. Even though he exhibited all of the traits of a pathological antagonist, he is still a human being.

Second, we must surrender our right to get even. I have often thought of various ways to get even with Jack. I have wanted simple revenge: He hurt me, so now I'll hurt him. I have even had many dreams, plotting acts of revenge. I have wanted to hurt him badly. I have reasoned, *He wrecked my career, my ministry, my health, my peace of mind, my marriage, which in turn ruined my future as I had then envisioned it; therefore, he should pay for his meanness.*

Third, Smedes continues, we must revise our feelings toward the person we forgive. Instead of feeling hatred for the offender, we gradually begin to wish the person well, hoping for his meanness to change to understanding and compassion. If this happens even slightly, we can be sure that God is working even a modest miracle of healing.

Through these steps, the abused clergyperson's wounds can heal. I am trying to see Jack for what he is—a failed human being, not greatly different from me or any other minister. I am trying to break "the vengeance addiction," surrendering the retaliation I once thought would bring me satisfaction. Moreover, I am trying to discover a grace in myself to hope that Jack "may still be given some crumbs off the table of grace to make his life livable." Smedes concludes that these three stages are "the fundamentals of the healing process."

What We Forgive

What do we forgive? Smedes suggests (1) we forgive persons, not institutions or organizations (for example, churches); (2) we forgive persons for what they do, not for what they are; (3) we forgive persons for what they do to seriously wound us; and (4) we forgive persons for what they do to wrong us when they wound us.[11]

Therefore, I need to forgive Jack, not the church that carelessly elected him and allowed him to get away with his unjust cruelty. I need to forgive Jack for blatantly lying about me; for accusing me of actions that I had not done; for masterminding a campaign to terminate me; for causing me such distress that my health was seriously affected; for pressuring me to take early retirement, which in turn resulted in having to sell my home and move to another state at considerable expense; for causing emotional distress and clinical depression that eventually resulted in the failure of an already weak marriage (some of the collateral damage referred to earlier); for being instrumental in turning several unsuspecting people against me for unfounded reasons; and for revising my entire future, something he had absolutely no right to do.

Also, I need to forgive Jack for what he did to seriously wound me. His actions were not trivial; they were serious and deadly. He severely wounded me mentally, emotionally, relationally, vocationally, and physically. I need to forgive Jack for the deep inner pain and boiling resentment I have struggled with for over six years. This pain is described by Smedes as "the reactive pain of frustrated fury."[12]

Finally, I need to forgive Jack for what he did to wrong me when he wounded me. There is suffering and then there is wrongful suffering. When a minister is fired for stealing money from his church, he will rightfully suffer for his thievery, but when a minister is run off for unjustifiable reasons, he will experience wrongful pain.

Jack's wrong was compounded because it almost sapped me, the violated person, of the courage or the will to trust anyone again. This is why it is so difficult for wounded ministers to remain in the ministry. Pastoral relationships call for trust, which holds personal relationships together. Pathological antagonists and clergy killers are in effect trust busters. When they succeed in destroying trust between a minister and his people, they destroy the "fellowship of the Spirit," and that is nothing short of moral evil. So I need to forgive Jack of this moral wrong he did to me.

Moreover, Smedes teaches that forgiving does not mean reunion. Forgiving Jack does not mean that I should welcome him back into my special circle of friends and family. I can care about him, maybe even work with him in the same church, but I don't have to live with him and restore him to a relationship that completely ignores the harm he inflicted. Rather, Smedes argues that forgiveness happens inside the person who gives it; forgiveness is not about reunion; forgiveness does not obligate us to go back. Smedes asks his readers to consider the following contrasts:

> It takes one person to forgive.
> It takes two to be reunited.
> Forgiving happens inside the wounded person.
> Reunion happens in a relationship between two people.
> We can forgive a person who never says he is sorry.
> We cannot be truly reunited unless he is honestly sorry.
> We can forgive even if we do not trust the person who wronged us once not to wrong us again.
> Reunion can happen only if we can trust the person who wronged us once not to wrong us again.
> Forgiving has no strings attached.
> Reunion has several strings attached.[13]

Who Forgives

Then Smedes asks, "Who qualifies to exercise forgiveness?" To qualify for forgiving, Smedes notes that we need only to meet three requirements.

Bearing Our Wounds

We need to bear the wounds ourselves. No one else can do our forgiving.

Recognizing the Wrong

We need to know we have been wronged. There is a difference in being a hurt person and being a wronged person. Some people are hurt over silly slights. One retired minister in my last pastorate took offense because I chose not to ask him to preach for me every time I was absent. A lady in our church got angry when I did not rush up to her after services and give her a warm hug of welcome each Sunday. She and her husband eventually moved to another church. It was not until after they left our church that she told me why. I had no idea she expected that kind of attention. To qualify as a forgiver, one needs to know that what he suffered, he suffered unfairly, that he has not just been hurt but has been morally wronged as well.

Feeling the Nudge

Then Smedes states that we need an inner push or nudge to forgive. Some people are easy forgivers, but most of us have to work at it. I do not find forgiveness easy. I need an inner reason for forgiving someone. It isn't enough to believe that I have an obligation to forgive or because the Bible says I should. The nudge to forgive must come from inside me as a desire from the heart. "*Wanting to* is the steam that pushes the forgiving engine," Smedes declares. What makes us want to? Smedes perceptively proclaims:

> We forgive when we feel a strong wish to be free from the pain that glues us to a bruised moment of the past. . . . We forgive when we feel God's Spirit nudging us with an impulse to pull ourselves out of the sludge of our disabling resentment. We forgive when we are ready to move toward a future unshackled from a painful past we cannot undo."[14]

The Fairness of Forgiveness

Some people consider forgiveness morally unfair. They believe it is psychologically dishonest and goes against human nature and that only moral wimps do it. Some would question the practical wisdom of forgiveness. And perhaps it *isn't* practical or even wise from the world's perspective. But from God's perspective it is the best choice for the Christian. Forgiving someone does not mean that you have forgotten how the person wronged you. Forgiveness helps you let go of that wrong and move on.

Smedes's case for forgiveness involves his conviction that forgiving an offender is an action that reflects the nature and character of God, and that it fits or suits the highest levels of human nature. Moreover, it is God's way of healing us from the hangover of a wounded past. It is a simple fact of life that forgiveness does more good for the forgiver than for the forgiven. Unforgiveness carries a special pain of bitterness and resentment that is extremely detrimental to one's physical, emotional, and spiritual welfare. To forgive the offender is to free oneself from this ongoing pain.[15]

I strongly recommend that every wounded minister read and ponder Lewis Smedes's *The Art of Forgiving*. An abused-clergy support group could well use this outstanding work as background reading. It has done me a world of good in the steps I am taking toward healing.

Christian pastoral psychologists William R. Miller and Kathleen A. Jackson have proposed a helpful set of theses regarding the meaning of forgiveness.[16] They say that retained anger signifies a failure to forgive and so takes on special meaning from a religious perspective. People often fail to forgive because they confuse forgiveness with any of five other matters, all of which it is not.

1. *Forgiveness is not the same as amnesia.* It is not forgetting and does not require it. One cannot forgive that which has already been forgotten. Rather, forgiveness is given in the face of remembering, and then forgiveness enables us to forget. Forgetting is no prerequisite, and to forgive does not require that we forget, a very difficult thing to do.
2. *Forgiveness is not acquittal,* finding the offender blameless and without responsibility. Rather, forgiveness is only required when the responsibility of the offender is recognized.
3. *Forgiveness is not an award,* something earned or given to those most deserving. Forgiveness must be given freely, without regard to merit.
4. *Forgiveness is not approval of an action or agreement with it.* It does not mean that the forgiving person is admitting that the offense was okay. In fact forgiveness is needed only when

the offended does not approve; it is given in the face of disapproval of the behavior.

5. *Forgiveness is not acquiescence.* This is no license for the forgiven to go and do as he pleases in the future. There is no moratorium here on values or a suspension of rules. This is not a permit to repeat the offense. Rather, in a mysterious way forgiveness inspires and empowers change. It is given in the face of the knowledge that the future may or may not be any different, but it is also given with the hope that it will.

From a positive perspective, Miller and Jackson define *forgiveness* as "an affirming acceptance of the *person* as distinguished from her or his actions. . . . It is also . . . a reflection of that profound kind of love that is attributed to God. Forgiveness is an alternative to anger. Better still, forgiveness is a *response* to anger."[17] Moreover, forgiveness reproduces itself. The forgiven are thereby enabled to forgive.

If a wounded minister does not learn the art of forgiving and thus experience the healing of his soul, then that minister will experience additional wounds to body, mind, and relationships. The toxicity of unforgiveness spreads relentlessly throughout one's life.

The Only Way

When I felt so wounded, I needed to find a closer walk with God. At first, this was very difficult to do. I was so angry, so bitter, so depressed that I decided that God really didn't care what happened to me. But I was wrong. God did care. He has proved it to me innumerable times since then. He has renewed my ministry in a new direction. Financially, I am stronger than ever. My personal life is happier than it has ever been. I can say without any reservations, God has been immeasurably good to me. He has taught me how to grow through, not around, the pain of rejection. I feel released from the past. I feel free to serve again.

To put it another way, I discovered that forgiveness is the bridge over which a wounded minister can move from the anger and resentment of the past to the freedom of a renewed ministry and walk with Christ. Forgiveness is also the road to a deeper faith regarding the nature and purpose of God in our lives. Learning to forgive my abusers taught me more about God's forgiveness than any book I ever read or lecture or sermon I ever heard. Only the forgiven can truly forgive, as Paul wrote, "forgiving one another as God in Christ has forgiven you" (Eph. 4:32).

I have described in this chapter the steps toward healing. Expect your healing to take time. You will need help through both individual and group therapy. Since this type of assistance often requires some expense, concerned laypersons might band together to provide such financial resources for their wounded minister to afford such help.

13 Recovering from Shattered Dreams

I know the experience of being forced out of a pastoral post at a most vulnerable age. In my early 60's I was not ready either emotionally or financially to retire. I felt that I was at the peak level of my ministerial skills. My education and experience qualified me to perform at a high level. My performance record spoke for itself.

Stigmas of Termination and Age

In the United States in the 1990s few if any churches or colleges would be willing to employ a man in his early sixties. The young have a distinct advantage. Why do churches and colleges tend to consider younger persons better qualified than older ones? They will never admit the real reasons, e.g., the young seemingly have more energy to throw into their work, you can hire them at a lower level of salary and benefits, and since these institutions are having a hard time reaching their youthful constituents, they believe that younger leaders can best reach and retain the young. So what does an unemployed sixty-two-year-old minister do? Well, he certainly has to be creative. Few if any of his contacts will come immediately to his rescue.

One thing he may do is go into clinical depression. It is a deeply discouraging feeling to be highly qualified from every recognized criteria of competency and be unsuccessful in finding employment. How are you supposed to feel when you have given your life to the church and/or its academic counterparts and find yourself stigmatized or fired because you are "too old" or were "a problem" in your last position? Well, for one thing, your early dreams of kingdom service for God become quickly shattered. Your perception of reality is that either God has gone fishing or has lost your address. This is not a pity party but a pity nightmare.

Similar feelings are experienced by wounded ministers of younger ages as well. Often when an investigating pastor search committee considers a terminated minister, they automatically assume the worst about him. Why is it assumed that the terminating church was probably in the right?

Most of these servants of God are lying wounded on the battlefield of ministry calling out "medic! medic!" and few if any come to help bind up their wounds. No wonder so many of them are bitter, cynical, discouraged, and depressed. No wonder so many of them "die" on the battlefield of service (i.e., they leave the ministry, maybe even the church altogether). Why is the secular military so much more concerned and effective in rescuing its wounded than God's church is in rescuing its wounded ministers? It is very difficult to overcome these stigmas of termination and age.

If you are a wounded minister, how can you recover from your shattered dreams, those deep scars of disillusionment over having been driven out of a ministry position? Here are several suggestions that I have discovered to be practical and necessary.

Restrengthen Your Faith in God

Let's be honest. Many wounded ministers are prone to experience a weakening of their faith in God when they have been rejected by a church. The experience of forced termination at least knocks the wind out of their faith. I am not saying that they believe they have lost their salvation. They simply do not understand why God seems to be so absent, so silent, so uninterested in their crisis. Their ministry crisis becomes a crisis of faith.

The Bible is replete with examples of depressed servants of God who, when they were at their lowest, recovered their confidence in God. A few reminders will suffice.

Elijah had been through a great victory over the priests of Baal when the wicked woman Jezebel sought to terminate the prophet.

In fear he ran for his life to Beer-sheba and into the wilderness to sit in despair under a broom tree. But an angel of the Lord appeared to him and encouraged him to go on to Horeb, the mount of God. There in a cave, God spoke to him, "What are you doing here, Elijah?" Elijah's answer contained words of fear and depression: "Everyone has forsaken your covenant; I alone am left." But God replied with a new commission for the prophet. He told him to anoint new leaders for Israel for a new day that was dawning. Out of this experience a new era for Israel began with a new prophet, Elisha, to lead them (read 1 Kings 18–19 for the full story). Elijah's faith in God was restrengthened.

Most if not all of the prophets experienced rejection and sometimes death at the hands of their own people, as both Jesus (Matt. 5:10–12) and Stephen (Acts 7:51–53) remind us. The abuse of the prophets came from within the ranks of the "people of God." God's reaction is vividly revealed by the chronicler as "the wrath of the LORD . . . so great that there was no remedy" since the people "kept mocking the messengers of God, despising his words, and scoffing at his prophets" (2 Chron. 36:16).

From the Davidic Psalter come the words of disillusionment of a depressed poet with which any wounded minister can identify:

> O LORD, do not rebuke me in your anger,
> or discipline me in your wrath.
> Be gracious to me, O LORD, for I am languishing;
> O LORD, heal me, for my bones are shaking with terror.
> My soul also is struck with terror,
> while you, O LORD—how long?
>
> Turn, O LORD, save my life;
> deliver me for the sake of your steadfast love.
> For in death there is no remembrance of you;
> in Sheol who can give you praise?
>
> I am weary with my moaning;
> every night I flood my bed with tears;
> I drench my couch with my weeping.
> My eyes waste away because of grief;
> they grow weak because of all my foes.

Depart from me, all you workers of evil,
  for the LORD has heard the sound of my weeping.
The LORD has heard my supplication;
  the LORD accepts my prayer.
All my enemies shall be ashamed and struck with terror;
  they shall turn back, and in a moment be put to shame.

Psalm 6

Is there any better example of rejection by a congregation than when Jesus himself was thrown out of his own synagogue at Nazareth? Yes, Jesus' preaching ministry at Nazareth was ended by "forced termination," whereby some of the synagogue leaders were filled with so much rage that they wanted to kill him by throwing him off a cliff. They would not accept his all-inclusive gospel that invited even Gentiles to faith (Luke 4:16–30). They thought they knew better than the Son of God what message they needed to hear.

And what wounded minister can forget the experience and words of Jesus himself as he was dying on the cross? There he prayed the words of Psalm 22: "My God, my God, why have you forsaken me?" (Matt. 27:46). Then on the third day his confidence in his heavenly Father was restored as he was raised from the dead. Wounded ministers readily identify with Jesus on the cross. They should also just as readily identify with him in his resurrection.

In addition, the apostle Paul and his associates were sometimes run out of town if not stoned and left for dead by stubborn and angry listeners (Acts 13:50; 14:1–20). Sometimes they were thrown into prison (Acts 16:16–40). In city after city they faced opposition and rejection. Paul also defends himself to the Corinthians against his opponents there by referring to these earlier experiences of abuse and rejection (2 Cor. 11:23–33).

Those who opposed him at Corinth actually were stalking him in order to discredit his message and ministry.[1] These "false apostles" were little different from what we earlier described as pathological antagonists and clergy killers who stimulated Paul to write what some scholars call his "harsh letter" (see 2 Corinthians 10–13). Time and again Paul experienced rejection by his own people, the Israelites (see Acts 21:27–36 for a noteworthy example in the temple precincts).

Paul often warned various congregations of pathological antagonists entering their ranks to cause trouble, alerting them that "savage wolves will come in among you, not sparing the flock" (Acts 20:29). So wounded ministers should not be surprised when this happens to them today.

The apostle Peter likewise warned elders and shepherds of the church of devilish opposition to their leadership. When he wrote, "Discipline yourselves, keep alert. Like a roaring lion your adversary the devil prowls around, looking for someone to devour" (1 Peter 5:8), he was referring to antagonism from within the church as well as from without. Peter went on to admonish, "Resist him, steadfast in your faith, for you know that your brothers and sisters in all the world are undergoing the same kinds of suffering" (1 Peter 5:9). Then he announced the great promise of hope: "And after you have suffered for a little while, the God of all grace, who has called you to his eternal glory in Christ, will himself restore, support, strengthen, and establish you" (1 Peter 5:10).

It is quite obvious from these biblical examples that God's ministers have always had to face some degree of opposition and antagonism. Even though it is natural to experience a diminishing degree of confidence in God when in the midst of such trials, it is also important for wounded ministers to recover their confidence in their heavenly Father to lead them beyond such devastating and traumatic rejection.

Allow these biblical examples, along with a deeper commitment to prayer, Bible study, and fasting, to restrengthen your faith. You may find yourself stronger than before you were wounded.

Listen Again to Your Call to Ministry

To recover his faith and confidence in God, a wounded minister needs desperately to listen again to his call to ministry. I personally have had to go back again to relive my initial call to the ministry or I would not have survived at all. I revisited the memories of my days in college when God first called me. At that time, at age nineteen, I believed that God was calling me to the preaching and pastoral ministry. I knew of nothing else in ministry. But as the years rolled by, it became apparent to me that God's call was much broader than pastoring a church. For several years I served as a teacher, first in a couple of Christian colleges and later in a theological seminary. However, along the way I had received special training and experience in pastoral counseling, so that at age sixty-two and unemployed as a pastor I made myself available to certain churches to serve as a pastoral counselor under their umbrella of sponsorship. I organized a nonprofit corporation called The Panhandle Pastoral Counseling Ministry for contracting with churches to perform their counseling services. Two large churches here in the Texas panhandle contracted with me to be their counselor. I was also offered an adjunct professorship to teach at a local branch of a Christian college. That is what I have been doing for the past six years, and I have more than enough work to do.

My call to ministry was again redirected, not canceled. I seldom preach anymore, but then I really have neither the time nor energy to do so. Instead, I teach preaching and theology to preachers at the local college branch, and I have found a new outlet for the gospel in the counseling room (not that I "preach" to clients but I help them "hear the gospel" in their search for answers to their personal and family problems). Clinical Christian counseling with individuals, couples, and families can minister just as deeply and effectively as a pulpit ministry can, I have come to believe.

You will recall the story of Moses being told to cast down his rod and God transformed it into a snake, then the snake became a rod again when Moses obeyed God's command to pick up the snake (Exod. 4:1–5). I vividly remember hearing pianist/composer/singer Ken Medema's first rendition of that story in his song "The Rod of God," especially as he sang the climax with the words, "The rod of Moses became the rod of God."

Wounded minister, what is your rod—what talent, gift, or ability do you have there in your hand, heart, or head? Throw it down. Give it to God. Let him transform it, and let it become the rod of God. There are all kinds of people in society who are in various kinds of bondage. They need another Moses to lead them into the "promised land" of freedom. You may have a preaching rod or a teaching rod or an administrative rod or a counseling rod or a computer rod or some other kind of ministry rod. Give it to God. For some the call will remain the same; for others there will be a new direction in ministry. It may take time and even some new training for updating your skills, but don't simply give up. Anyone can give up. The world is full of washed out wounded ministers who did that. Don't join their pathetic ranks.

If your call was valid and real in the beginning, it is still valid and real today. It may simply need reworking, redirecting, and renewal.

Your future in God's plans may not include a position on a church staff. The ministry is so varied today. You have to find your own niche in kingdom service. However, whatever you do vocationally, a minister needs to be affiliated and personally involved in a local church, just as any other Christian. Wounded ministers are prone to believe that "church is a place where you get hurt." But just because you were hurt deeply in one church doesn't mean that all churches will hurt you. I have experienced that, although I was hurt in one church, I have found healing in another church. If you have any future in ministry, it will require that you get involved in a local church even if it is in a voluntary form of service, for example, teaching a Bible class or directing a visitation program. There is no future in ministry for a wounded minister who lies around doing nothing, feeling sorry for himself.

Be Creative

Be creative in allowing God to redirect your ministry. There are possibilities in today's society that you may never have dreamed about. Surf the Internet. Study the course offerings in local college catalogues. Look at the continuing education offerings of area theological seminaries. Read through recent issues of Christian journals and magazines. Visit local Christian bookstores and peruse the recent published works regarding the Christian ministry. From these sources, several possibilities may "ring your ministry bell."

Seek vocational counseling. Call your denominational headquarters or service agencies to locate this special type of counseling. Turn to nearby fellow ministers you know and trust for counsel. Knowledgeable laypersons can also be of assistance. Some licensed professional counselors are specially trained in vocational counseling. Some counseling centers are equipped with specialists who can give tests to determine vocational interests and potential adeptness. Don't be ashamed to ask others to share their ideas about your possible vocational future.

Proverbs offers encouragement here: "Where there is no guidance, a nation falls, but in an abundance of counselors there is safety" (11:14); "Wise warriors are mightier than strong ones, and those who have knowledge than those who have strength; for by wise guidance you can wage your war, and in abundance of counselors there is victory" (24:5–6).

Having found intelligent Christian counseling for my situation, I was able to reflect on, with personal application, the words of the psalmist's confidence in the Lord's leading: "I [God] will instruct you and teach you the way you should go; I will counsel you with my eye upon you" (Ps. 32:8). And then looking back on the help I received in counseling, I could say, "You guide me with your counsel, and afterward you will receive me with honor" (Ps. 73:24).

Retooling

After counsel you may need to retool for a new ministry direction. This may require learning computer skills. (Someone once said, "The new poor of the twenty-first century will be the computer illiterates.") Moreover, it never hurts to improve your speaking skills by taking a speech or communications course at a nearby college. Also, look around for special courses dealing with raising your self-esteem, which is probably at a low level currently.[2] Having had your vocational dreams shattered nearly always includes having your self-esteem shattered as well.

You may be saying to yourself, "I'm too old to go back to college or seminary and retool for ministry." But this happens all the time in the secular world. Many middle-aged persons have chosen to leave one profession and retool for another. When I was a seminary professor, I well recall that many of our students were persons over forty who had come out of one career to enter the ministry. They had been lawyers, teachers, medical specialists, businesspeople, bankers, or investors. They felt the hand of God leading them in a new direction. You can do the same.

Revise Your Résumé

After retooling for a new ministry direction, revise your personal vocational résumé. Get a professional to help you. Ask around. Someone in your city or area knows how to prepare a résumé that looks professionally done. Or use a computer program for this. Your résumé is a projection of who you are, what you have done, and what you can do. Always include a professional photograph of yourself. Appearances say a lot about character, class, and style.

Distribute your résumé to ministry sources and agencies that are in touch with vocational opportunities. This would include denominational job-placement offices, often located in denominational agencies, universities, and seminaries. Quality schools will usually want to assist their graduates.

Wait on God

In the meantime, as previously noted, devote your time, energy, and skills to the ministry of some local church just as any dedicated Christian would do. Then pray and wait for God to lead.

In all of the above, you will be proving yourself and earning the respect of others. No one will respect and want someone who projects a defeatist attitude, who feels sorry for himself, who exhibits self-pity, who has given up and quit doing anything constructive for himself or others. Imagine yourself on a search committee for a church or agency. Would you want someone like you to be an example for and lead others? If not, then get your act together. God uses those who are already doing something constructive about themselves and for others. Wait on and trust God but act on your instincts led by the Spirit.

Start a New Ministry

One suggestion that may seem radical for some people is to consider the possibility of starting a new work of ministry. This is exactly what the apostle Paul did. It is the work of the missionary—initiating a new ministry where none has existed before. It is true that in many communities there are already plenty of churches, maybe too many in some cases. But in many more communities there just may be a need for a new evangelical church.

Since it appears that most wounded ministers are abused in older, established churches that have stagnated in growth, maybe your ministry could best flourish in beginning a new congregation that would look on you as their founding minister. You could organize it without the traditional built-in hazards of power struggles, such as a self-perpetuating board of deacons or official board. Instead of a board of deacons or elders, why not a ministry of deacons structured to render service to the congregation as the first deacons were established to do in the early church (Acts 6:1–7)? You could set up a ministers' advisory council as suggested earlier in this book, not only to advise but to protect the ministers from any antagonists that might come along in the future.

Many new churches are started with denominational endorsement and even financial support. If your background is in a denomination, then this may be your best approach. However, the wave of the future seems to be a nondenominational ministry, which is independent of denominational control or influence.

Even a growing number of traditional Baptist churches have chosen not to use the denominational label "Baptist" in their name. Rather, they are going the direction of the community church identity. Examples are West Side Church in Omaha, Nebraska, The Church of Los Colinas in Dallas, Texas, and Saddleback Valley Community Church, in California. All of these are large and growing Southern Baptist churches.

Robert Schuller's Crystal Cathedral was originally called the Garden Grove Community Church in Orange County, California, but from its beginning this huge congregation has been officially affiliated with the Reformed Church in America (originally the Dutch Reformed Church). A church's denominational identity does not have to be included in its name. Many avant-garde church growth specialists argue that it is better not to be publicly identified with a particular denomination, especially if the church is trying to win the masses of unchurched people who have no denominational background and/or who might have a negative attitude toward denominational labels.

In addition to starting a new church, there are other possible new ministries that you could initiate: a prison or jail ministry, a retirement home ministry, a rescue ministry for transients or addicted persons, a truck-stop ministry for truckers, and if you have the training and credentials, a pastoral counseling ministry. The possibilities are almost endless. Often various denominational agencies sponsor many different types of new ministries.

As you exercise your unique creativity to redirect your ministry away from a wounded minister experience, plan to succeed. I say this because any new ministry you begin will be difficult, and there may be setbacks along the way. Keep your eyes on your ultimate goal—to succeed, not to fail. I once heard Robert Schuller in a leadership conference in his church say, "We cannot afford to fail; there are too many people out there counting on us to succeed because they are desperately in need of our ministry."[3]

Revise Any Dysfunctional Core Beliefs

The best way to plan to succeed is to examine your personality and get rid of any seeds of failure. This requires that you know what your core beliefs are and revise any that are dysfunctional. Seeds of failure are core beliefs that predetermine that you will not succeed in reaching your ministry goals. Examples are: I am a loser; I cannot do anything right; People will not like me; I am ugly and repulsive; My life is doomed to failure; I will be rejected by people when they really get to know me; I am a victim—bad things just happen to me; No one really loves me.

Cognitive therapy identifies core beliefs as those that are deep in the core of one's personality and are usually not consciously recognized.[4] Some core beliefs are functional; for example, I am a capable person; I am worth loving; My life is a beautiful gift from God; Most people will accept me when they really get to know me; A setback or a defeat can become an opportunity for growth; The future looks bright. But some core beliefs are dysfunctional and can become seeds of failure. Core beliefs produce what are called "automatic thoughts." Here is an example.

Two people live next door to each other. Both park their cars in their driveways. One morning both simultaneously discover that each has a flat tire. One shouts, "That's just my luck; bad things are always happening to me," while he kicks the grass and angrily changes his tire before going on to work, blaming that so-and-so who left a nail in the street.

The other person sees his flat tire and says, "Whoops, flat tire. I'm going to be late to work, so I'd better change it in a hurry; I have more important things to do at my job." He quickly changes his flat tire, gets to work late but explains to his boss what happened, and goes to his desk to start his work for the day.

What a difference in their "automatic thoughts" used to interpret the same experience! The first person interpreted out of the core belief, *I am a victim.* The second interpreted out of the opposite core belief, *I am a victor.* The first interpreted the situation as, *Bad things happen to me,* while the second interpreted the same predicament as, *I can handle this; I have more important things to do.*

Cognitive therapists also suggest that dysfunctional core beliefs are the results of distorted thinking. Dr. David Burns lists the following possibilities:

1. *All-or-nothing thinking.* You look at things in absolute, black-and-white categories.
2. *Overgeneralization.* You view a negative event as a never-ending pattern of defeat.
3. *Mental filter.* You dwell on the negatives and ignore the positives.
4. *Discounting the positives.* You insist that your accomplishments or positive qualities don't count.
5. *Jumping to conclusions.* You conclude things are bad without any definite evidence. Two types are:
   Mind reading. You assume that people are reacting negatively to you.
   Fortune-telling. You predict that things will turn out badly.
6. *Magnification or minimization.* You blow things way out of proportion or you shrink their importance.
7. *Emotional reasoning.* You reason from how you feel: "I feel like an idiot, so I must be one."
8. *"Should" statements.* You criticize yourself or other people with *shoulds, shouldn'ts, musts, oughts,* and *have-tos.*
9. *Labeling.* Instead of saying, "I made a mistake," you tell yourself, "I'm a jerk" or "I'm a loser."

10. *Blame.* You blame yourself for something you weren't entirely responsible for, or you blame other people and overlook ways that you contributed to a problem.[5]

Let's apply this approach to Pastor Gerald who was terminated by his church for several reasons, none of which were moral or theological. His first thoughts were: *I'm a born loser; I'll never get another job; I'm letting my family down.* Taking his first thought, *I'm a born loser,* let's apply the above distorted thinking patterns to his reasoning.

- *All-or-nothing thinking.* Pastor Gerald is looking at himself in black-and-white categories. He sees himself only as a total loser.
- *Overgeneralization.* He lost his job, but he's generalizing to his entire self.
- *Mental filter.* He's dwelling on this bad event and letting it discolor his entire view of life, much like the drop of ink that discolors a beaker of water.
- *Discounting the positives.* He's overlooking his many good qualities.
- *Jumping to conclusions.* He automatically assumes that people are reacting negatively to him (mind reading), or he predicts that his situation will invariably turn out bad (fortune-telling); evidence is lacking for either conclusion.
- *Magnification or minimization.* He's blowing this negative event out of proportion.
- *Emotional reasoning.* Gerald reasons from how he feels. He feels like a born loser, so he believes he really is one!
- *"Should" statements.* He may have the belief that he should always be successful at things and never fail. He may also believe that if he is a good person and tries hard, life should always go smoothly.
- *Labeling.* He's labeling himself as "a born loser" instead of trying to learn from the situation or thinking about the best way to find a new position elsewhere.
- *Blame.* He's automatically blaming himself for being terminated. In point of fact, several pastors of his church have been

terminated in the past. Gerald's employment record has been excellent.[6]

Pastor Gerald can change the way he feels (defeated, rejected, useless, unwanted, a failure) by changing the way he *thinks*. For example, he could reason as follows:

- I have lost this job, but that's all I've lost. I still have my health, my family, my abilities, my calling, my future.
- I lost this job, but I'll find another one.
- This bad event of being terminated will not affect my entire view of life. From God's perspective, life is good.
- I have many good qualities and I can use my abilities elsewhere.
- This has not been a pleasant event, but it is not the end of my ministry.
- I may have lost this particular job, but I am not a born loser.
- It is only realistic that life at times will have its failures and not always run smoothly for me.
- I am still a good, though not perfect, minister, so what can I learn from this experience? And how can I find a new position elsewhere?
- It does no good to blame myself or others for what happened. It happened to some of my predecessors; why am I any different? This church has a history of terminating ministers, and I happen to be one of those so terminated. I will claim the promise of Romans 8:28, "We know that all things work together for good for those who love God, who are called according to his purpose." I must get on with my life and ministry wherever I can be accepted, respected, and appreciated.

Earlier I referred to core beliefs that are dysfunctional. These are beliefs of which we are not usually conscious, but they are deeply held and have a very powerful impact on our behavior. Wounded ministers are prone to hold to some of the following, which are dysfunctional (that is, they create problems in one's performance and interpersonal relationships):

1. I will be rejected in most situations.
2. I will fail in most endeavors.
3. I must be in control of most situations.
4. I need everyone's approval.
5. I feel responsible for others' feelings.
6. I feel like a victim in most situations.
7. I am a loser most of the time.
8. Love must be earned with some unusual accomplishments.
9. If things do not go as I have planned, I am out of control.
10. If others do not do as I wish, they do not care about me.
11. I must be strong (perfect, right), for only then will others care about me.
12. If anything goes wrong, it is usually my fault.
13. If others hurt me deeply, then I must punish them.
14. My opinions, plans, and beliefs must never be questioned by anyone.
15. Others are bound to reject me.
16. I must be the center of attention in most situations.
17. I am not really important unless I get my way.
18. It is awful if others don't approve of everything I do.
19. I am a bad person.
20. I'll never get better; I am doomed to my present misery.
21. I should always be happy.
22. Life should always be fair.
23. If I'm not on top, I'm a flop.
24. If I make a mistake, it means I am a failure.
25. If somebody disagrees with me, it means he or she doesn't like me.
26. Spiritual Christians will never have serious problems.
27. It is always best to assume the worst.
28. Others will attack (or criticize) me if I show a sign of weakness.
29. If people don't agree with me, it's because they do not think I am important or significant.
30. Criticism of me is always destructive to me.
31. Anger is always wrong.
32. Godly Christians will never be depressed.
33. Anyone who questions what I do is a bully.
34. If I don't get my way, I can choose anger as a way to control others.

This is only a partial list. I am sure there are many other dysfunctional core beliefs, but it should be readily apparent how any of the above can produce problematic interpretations of life situations, relationships, or events for ministers in a church ministry.

I will try to revise each of these into a more functional belief:

1. Although I don't deserve to be rejected, there may be times when I will be rejected by someone, and then I will try to find out why.
2. Although I am not a failure, there may be times when I will fail, and then I will try to learn from them.
3. I do not need to be in control of most situations; I will enlist others to assist me in my leadership duties. Besides, I trust God to be in control ultimately.
4. I do not need everyone's approval, only God's and my own.
5. Others are responsible for their own feelings as I am for mine.
6. I am a victor. I can say with Paul, "I can do all things through [Christ] who strengthens me" (Phil. 4:13).
7. I am capable most of the time of accomplishing what I need to do.
8. Love is a gift. It is not conditional or based on any accomplishments.
9. If things do not go as planned, I will seek counsel, revise my plans, and try again with new approaches.
10. If others do not do as I wish, then I assume they have their own good reasons, and I will try to learn from them.
11. I will be myself and then trust others to care about me because they want to do so.
12. If anything goes wrong, I will seek counsel, learn from the experience, but not beat up on myself by taking all the blame.
13. If others hurt me deeply, I will try to understand why and ask God's help to forgive them.
14. Others have a right to question my opinions, plans, and beliefs; maybe I can learn from them.
15. If others reject me, it may say more about them than it does about me; but I will try to understand why. I am not deserving of rejection; God accepts me unconditionally.
16. I do not need to be the center of attention; humility is the better stance in interpersonal relationships.

17. I am always important to God whether I get my way with others or not.
18. Others may not always approve of what I do; that is reality.
19. I am a sinner saved by grace and a saint in process.
20. God is in the process of growing me through whatever misery I may be experiencing at the present.
21. Happiness is a choice, but faithfulness to God is better.
22. Life is not always fair; that is reality.
23. If I'm not on top, I need to stop—and try to understand why I sometimes think I need to be. God is always on top, so why want his job?
24. If I make a mistake, I will try to learn from it and revise my actions.
25. If someone disagrees with me, I assume he or she has good reasons, and I may be able to learn from them.
26. Spiritual Christians will sometimes have serious problems; they are not immune to them.
27. One should always assume the best about people, not the worst. Give people the benefit of the doubt.
28. Others may attack (criticize) me; it is a part of the human territory, but maybe I can learn from the criticism.
29. My importance or significance is not determined by whether others agree with me or not. If I am important to God, that is enough.
30. Criticism goes with being human; it may say more about the critic than it does me; I will try to learn from it, make necessary corrections, then get on with my life.
31. Anger is neither right nor wrong. There are no right or wrong feelings; there are just feelings. Anger does need to be managed or controlled.
32. Godly Christians may sometimes be depressed; some of the great saints of the past experienced depression. Depression needs treatment, not condemnation.
33. Anyone who questions what I do may be a bully, but it is not wise to classify all of my opponents as bullies. Sometimes they may be my friends.[7]
34. If I don't get my way, I will not choose the counterproductive method of anger, but will choose to understand, empathize, be compassionate, and seek counsel from wise confidants.

I recommend that you identify your dysfunctional core beliefs, using the above guidelines along with counseling, and revise them into positive core beliefs as I have illustrated above. If you want to recover from your shattered dreams, this is a place to begin. Your core beliefs determine how you interpret life's experiences, situations, and relationships. You have little or no control over life's painful experiences, but you do have control over the way you interpret and respond to them.

So, in summary, events do not create feelings; thoughts do. Your thoughts about an event are your interpretation of it. What determines the way you interpret an event is one or more of your core beliefs. To repeat, an event in your life is interpreted a certain way, which in turn generates your feelings about it, which in turn produces your behavior in reaction to it. Your interpretation is determined by your core beliefs.

Therefore, to change your dysfunctional feelings and behavior, you have to challenge and change those core beliefs that are dysfunctional into core beliefs that are functional. As a Christian, I believe that functional core beliefs are those that are in harmony with biblical truth and reality. These beliefs are particularly in keeping with the spirit, attitude, and behavior exhibited in the life and ministry of Jesus Christ.

With understanding, practice, prayer, and counsel, a wounded minister can recover from his shattered dreams of ministry woundedness by following this method. It has worked for me. I hope it will work for you.

14 Wounded Healers

I have discovered that God can use my woundedness as a minister to become a wounded healer for other abused ministers. It goes without saying that there are many of us. Some careful observers are calling this problem "epidemic." Lloyd Rediger begins his study of this crisis as follows:

> Abuse of pastors by congregations and the breakdown of pastors due to inadequate support are now tragic realities. This worst-case scenario for the church, one that is increasing in epidemic proportions, is not a misinterpretation by a few discontented clergy. Rather, it is a phenomenon that is verified by both research and experience.

So what is being done about this tragedy by major church leaders? Rediger continues:

> Worse yet, there is a strong tendency toward denial of this reality in denominational offices and among clergy who have not yet been forced out of their congregations or battered emotionally and spiritually while trying to be faithful pastors.[1]

Denial or underestimation of the problem by those who should know better and who are in a position to do something about it mean that the only ones left in a position to do something constructive and redemptive about clergy abuse are the abused clergy themselves. These are the persons who are uniquely experienced to become wounded healers of the abused.

What Is a Wounded Healer?

The concept of a wounded healer came several years ago from Henri J. M. Nouwen, Roman Catholic scholar who was then teaching at Yale Divinity School. His book *The Wounded Healer* is now a classic. The title was suggested in an old legend Nouwen found in the Talmud, the collection of ancient rabbinic writings that make up the basis of religious authority for traditional Judaism. The legend is this:

> Rabbi Yoshua ben Levi came upon Elijah the prophet while he was standing at the entrance of Rabbi Simeron ben Yohai's cave. . . . He asked Elijah, "When will the Messiah come?"
> Elijah replied, "Go and ask him yourself."
> "Where is he?"
> "Sitting at the gates of the city."
> "How shall I know him?"
> "He is sitting among the poor covered with wounds. The others unbind all their wounds at the same time and then bind them up again. But he unbinds one at a time and binds it up again, saying to himself, 'Perhaps I shall be needed: if so I must always be ready so as not to delay for a moment.'"[2]

The story reveals that the Messiah is to be found among the poor, needy, and injured, binding his own wounds one at a time, anticipating the moment when his healing care will be needed. So it can be with wounded ministers who are trying to grow spiritually and emotionally through their experiences of abuse. They must look after their own wounds but at the same time be ready to offer healing support to other wounded ministers.

Your wounds, inflicted by pathological antagonists and clergy killers, can be filled with purpose and meaning as you reach out to other wounded ministers to help heal their injured spirits. It actually facilitates your own healing when you take your eyes off yourself and focus on the injuries of others in the ministry.

Familiar examples of wounded healers in secular society are those who are involved in Alcoholics Anonymous, Al-Anon, and Alateen family groups, Gamblers Anonymous, Codependents Anonymous, Mothers Against Drunk Driving, Narcotics Anonymous, Overeaters Anonymous, and Compassionate Friends (parents who have lost a child in death). Why not a Wounded Ministers Anonymous (or Abused Clergy Anonymous) organization?

An Ongoing Support Group

You may be the only wounded minister you know about in your town, city, or county, but there are probably others unknown to you. Start by calling around to other ministers in your circle of acquaintances, explain to them your idea, and invite them to an initial meeting. Let the membership be clearly interdenominational.

Invite these contacts and their spouses to a light supper meeting in your home. At that meeting, identify the problem and discuss the idea of a monthly support group. I say monthly since most ministers will resist another meeting on a weekly basis in their already busy schedule. After the group begins meeting, it might be decided that meeting more often would be both desirable and helpful. Meet in homes, rotating among members. It is more comfortable and informal to meet in a home. Refreshments are optional but desirable. Measure the interest of the group. If there are three or more who are interested, get started. You don't need to have a large number to start with. The people at the initial meeting will know of others to invite to subsequent meetings. Don't forget those wounded ministers who are not currently employed on an active church staff. Even then, keep the size of the group to no more than a dozen. Ask the initial group to select a leader who will fearlessly take charge with a sense of mission to provide healing for emotionally battered clergy. The group will require a strong leader/convener who isn't afraid of what others will think of his situation, who isn't afraid to share his pain, and who can readily identify with any wounded minister with genuine empathy. The leader needs to be familiar with small-group dynamics and might even be a paid professional who understands the role of a minister in a church setting.

Do some background reading on support groups.[3] Another way to learn about the power of support groups is to attend some of the open meetings of Alcoholics Anonymous and Al-Anon. These folks are the real professionals in the healing power of support

215

groups. I attend their meetings regularly just to learn from them. They will also indirectly teach you that the wounded minister is not alone among the many different types of walking wounded.

In the initial meeting, tell your own story of woundedness. The others will likely identify with you readily. Explain your feeling of a sense of need for the support and encouragement a group could give. Suggest the following ground rules to facilitate the functioning of the group:

1. The group will meet once a month (or more often if desired) at an agreed-on time and day, preferably during the evening so that spouses who work outside the home can attend as well.
2. Members must commit themselves to the group as a significant priority, and to the meeting time, allowing nothing else to prevent attendance (short of illness or an emergency).
3. Members will take turns hosting the group in their homes.
4. One member will be recognized as leader/convener, who will preside, although this person must be careful not to dominate the group's discussions. This person will open and close each meeting, keep the group on track, make assignments if and when a book is to be studied (always to be read in advance), and establish the next meeting place at the end of each meeting.
5. *Anything* a person discusses in a group session is to be considered strictly *confidential,* never to be mentioned outside of the group to anyone else. This is absolutely necessary if members are to feel free to talk within the group.
6. Group sessions must begin on time and end on time. If some want to stay longer, they may, but others need to feel free to leave; some may need to relieve babysitters.
7. The group will establish calendar boundaries as well (for example, September 1 to May 31). Some flexibility needs to be allowed during certain weeks when the group may not meet (especially around Christmas and Easter).
8. Each member should make a covenant agreement to pray for every other member each day.

As to an agenda for each session, be flexible, but have some ideas in mind. During the first couple of meetings, the group's purpose and ground rules need to be made clear, and time should be spent on getting acquainted. I have known some small groups that drew up a contract, including ground rules, and asked each participant to sign it as a pledge of commitment.

How long should such a group meet? I would suggest at least a six-month trial period to begin with, then evaluate the experience at the end of that period to determine the group's future.

Such a group is no cure-all, but it can be a means of encouragement, healing of emotions, and assistance as to future direction of its members. Some of the group's members may still be in an abusive situation where they are almost daily dealing with abusive persons, and they will need help in how to cope with these difficult people.

Background reading could be suggested to stimulate discussion and sharing during the group sessions. Possible resources are the books referenced earlier by Kenneth C. Haugk and G. Lloyd Rediger; or this book could be used. See the bibliography at the end of this book for other possibilities.

A One-on-One Ministry

If a support group is not feasible, due to distance or scheduling factors, then consider a one-on-one ministry with another wounded minister who is accessible. For several reasons, you may not be able to get a large enough group of interested ministers together, but maybe there is one person you could meet with on a regular basis. Possibly you could include a third minister who is older, more experienced, and is not currently hurting, or who may be retired. This minister could serve as a more objective, unbiased reflector for the other two of you.

In my current counseling practice, I sometimes find myself counseling a wounded minister who has nowhere else to turn. Just the two of us meet usually twice a month. Sometimes the minister's spouse meets with us. I know what they are going through. I can empathize with them. I am able to serve as a sounding board, a mentor, a reflector of their abusive situation, reflecting back their feelings, so they can better understand and manage their emotions. If nothing else, I try to be a supportive friend.

So look around in your community or county and try to find another minister you can relate to on a one-on-one basis, someone who understands the pain of ministerial woundedness, who can be objective with you, who also desires healing for his own wounds, and who is open to new directions for the future. You can be a lot of help to each other.

As a wounded minister, you need help to heal, but your goal in getting together with another wounded minister is the help you can give him. You'll find that playing the role of a wounded healer will enhance your own healing and encouragement.

Plan Wounded Ministers' Retreats

Southern Baptist evangelist Freddie Gage has been especially successful in providing leadership for occasional retreats for wounded ministers and their wives. Calling them Wounded Heroes retreats, Gage has spearheaded the only large-scale effort among Southern Baptists to minister to wounded clergy and their spouses. During 1998 and 1999, several of these five-day events were held nationwide, often drawing as many as one hundred people who have experienced some type of emotional abuse at the hands of a church or a small group in a church.

In early 1999 the Wounded Heroes retreat program was taken over by the Pastor-Staff Leadership Department of LifeWay Christian Resources, a Southern Baptist agency in Nashville, Tennessee. A special division of that department called LeaderCare now provides leadership and resources for the Wounded Heroes ministry. Those interested in more information about this ministry may call the LeaderCare office at 615-251-2265. The director is Dr. Brooks Faulkner (woundedheroes@lifeway.com). The retreats are open to people of all denominations.

The Wounded Heroes retreats in 1998 and 1999, held in Texas, Florida, Georgia, and North Carolina, were very successful. The one in Texas was held in Dallas in early 1998 at the famous Cooper Aerobics Center where Dr. Kenneth Cooper, the creator of aerobics, provided some of the leadership for the retreat. Licensed professional counselors were also brought in to assist with the retreat program. More than 1,400 ministers or their wives called for information about the retreat, but only 50 slots were available for participants. The waiting list reached 140. The *Dallas Morning News* published a major story in its religion section about this retreat.[4]

The cost of such retreats may vary. Freddie Gage estimated that his retreats cost an average of $1,875 per couple, but outside sources from various denominational agencies and gifts from individuals covered most of this. All speakers and facilitators donated their time and expenses.[5] Area church groups and denominational entities could probably secure funding for their own retreats, the cost being dependent on the location of the retreat, speakers and facilitators enlisted, and cost of administration.

Even though professional leadership was provided for Gage's retreats, post-retreat testimonies by participants revealed that the participants served as wounded healers for each other.[6] They identified with each other in a personal way. As each sought to bind up their own wounds, they in turn tried to bind up the others' wounds.

If you would like to initiate this type of retreat, talk with the denominational leaders of your district or state about assistance. If you are serving in a nondenominational church, talk with those in other independent churches about this type of ministry. Don't just sit back and feel sorry for yourself. Do something about it. Take some initiative. Become a wounded healer. You will find a close camaraderie among wounded ministers. Many will want to help organize a retreat and find funding for it. Compassionate laypersons will also want to help if they know what to do.

What are possible topics to cover in such a retreat? The original Wounded Heroes retreats were quite ambitious. Their topics included fear of failure, anger management techniques, how to deal with rejection, burnout prevention, conflict resolution, dysfunctional family life, depression, how to deal with stress, unfaithfulness, forgiveness, dumping emotional baggage from the past, life after termination, distorted views of God, home improvement suggestions, divorce-proofing your marriage, abuse (physical, verbal, emotional), spiritual abuse, surviving a fishbowl existence, what they don't teach you in seminary, being a pastor's wife and being yourself. Focus was also put on the wounded wives of wounded heroes as well as prodigal preachers' kids.

I would add the following topics: how to deal with cantankerous lay leaders (pathological antagonists and clergy killers) or bully pastors (if you are a staff associate) without losing your temper or your job, setting up the ministers' advisory council, overcoming bitterness after forced termination, how to avoid collateral damage to yourself and your family members (including various medical problems), and practical steps to take to find a new position after termination.

If you would like consultation regarding setting up a retreat, you can e-mail me at guyfg@msn.com. Also your own denominational regional, state, or national offices may provide assistance. There is currently no charge for any of these consultations.

Entirely too many wounded ministers are attempting to handle their pain alone. This isolation in misery is unnecessary. Others need your help. You may need help as well. If so, then rise up above your injuries and damaged ministry and pull together a group of like-minded wounded ministers and minister to each other. Follow in the steps of the master Wounded Healer. You will find this Wounded Healer at the gate of your city caring for the other wounded. He is inviting you to join him.

Afterword

Growing through Rejection

The most apparent emotion experienced by wounded ministers who have been abused in one way or another is *rejection*. It is extremely painful to be called to a church as a minister and then find yourself disliked, unwanted, and eventually asked to leave, or what's worse, being forcefully terminated with nowhere to go. This is especially true when such rejection is based on what so often appear to be trivial reasons. Even more difficult is termination over accusations that are vague or ambiguous, one of the most common being, "His sermons just don't feed us."

It would be something else to be terminated for biblical reasons: immorality, especially sexual, and heresy, that is, teachings opposed to the official doctrines of the Bible as interpreted by one's church. Most of the terminations I have studied in my research involved neither immorality nor heresy on the part of the terminated minister. Most of the terminations I have observed have been a rejection of the minister as a person. These terminations were usually instigated by a small group of lay leaders who simply didn't like the minister and his style of leadership. They rejected him and what he represented through his personality.

Such rejection is a direct attack on the minister's self-image, his sense of personhood, as well as his essential character. He is simply deemed unfit to be a minister of the church. Whether so deemed by one person, "the church boss," an oligarchy of powerful lay leaders, or the majority of the congregation in a church business session (probably influenced by a few antagonists), a rejected minister experiences an emotional reaction that is very painful and difficult to handle.

If this has been your experience, you as a wounded minister have two choices: Either you let the rejection destroy you in bitterness and resentment or you determine to grow through the experience. Assuming you really want to grow through the rejection, I make the following suggestions.

Stop Whining

First of all, it would help immensely if you would stop feeling sorry for yourself and stop whining about what happened to you. After what happened to me in my last pastorate, I struggled with clinical depression for the next two years, complaining to everyone who would listen to me about how horribly I was treated by that church. I wallowed in anger and resentment over being so abused. These negative emotions even destroyed my marriage, especially when my wife showed no sympathy for me, refusing to listen to me ventilate my feelings.

Incidentally, if you are the spouse of a rejected minister, decide now to be a good nonjudgmental listener. He simply needs you to listen to him verbalize his feelings. He doesn't need you to fix anything, even if you could. Just listen, and learn to reflect back what you hear so he will know you hear and understand. He is wounded, hurting, in deep pain, and he has a severely bruised ego. A church that once called him with enthusiasm in the context of a spiritual purpose has now rejected him and taken away his perceived reason for existing. Healing can only begin to take place when he feels free to begin the ventilation of these negative emotions to a caring ear. He also needs encouragement to find a competent professional counselor who will also listen to him. But his spouse needs to listen also.

But whining is something else. It is a pity party. It is feeling sorry for oneself. It is refusing to take responsibility for oneself. It is an attempt to blame everyone else for one's problems.

Rather, ask yourself, *What can I learn from this experience? How can I make this experience a means for my own spiritual growth? What can God teach me in the midst of what is happening to me?*

Being wounded by a church, even if the rejection is led by a pathological few, will in time reveal the content of the abused minister's character. In God's hands wounds are a means of healing others. It was Isaiah who wrote of the Messiah: "by his bruises we are healed" (Isa. 53:5). If we are truly servants of the Lord, should not our wounds also be a means of strengthening and healing others? We never find Jesus whining.

Do as Jesus did. When one city rejected him (as at Nazareth, Luke 4:28–30), he went on to other cities where the people would respect and listen to him. Recall that he also told his disciples: "If anyone will not welcome you or listen to your words, shake off the dust from your feet as you leave that house or town" (Matt. 10:14). Learn how to turn your rejection in one church into acceptance in another.

Start Over

It's time to begin again; start over. Back up and take a long, hard look at the big picture of your life. On the football field a winning team is made up of players who, when they are knocked down, get up and run the next play. They don't feel sorry for themselves and leave the field to go and play tennis or chess. Wounded ministers are players who have had the wind knocked out of them, tackled for a loss or a fumble, but their Coach calls them to get up and run another play. Quitting is not an option on God's team.

As in football, staying on the team may mean changing positions. I have moved from being a pastor to a new role in pastoral counseling, just as before I moved from being a pastor to teaching or from teaching to being a pastor. But I stayed on God's ministry team. I simply changed positions. In some instances, however, a pastor rejected by one church may become a pastor graciously accepted by a different church. You may still be on God's team but in a different location.

In other instances, before starting over, some wounded ministers may need to take a break for a time of healing. Of course, to do this they must consider financial resources. What do they do during this break time to be able to continue paying the bills? Also there may be moving expenses to consider. Therefore, a break may

223

mean some type of alternate work outside a local church, for example, school teaching, a position in business, counseling, or one of a variety of government jobs. A friend of mine left a heavily conflicted church situation and found a very rewarding counseling position with a state government agency that works with delinquent youth, and yet he continues to serve churches as an interim pastor. This provided a wounded minister an opportunity to heal before accepting another full-time pastoral position.

It should not be surprising to find that Jesus sometimes directed his disciples to take a break from stressful situations (see Mark 6:30–32). This principle should be applied to any wounded minister to enable him to experience a healthy recovery.

Deepen Your Faith by Forgiving

The wounds inflicted by rejection can be healed only by exercising the divine gift of forgiveness, which in turn works to deepen the faith of the wounded person. In recent years much has been learned by many in the medical profession and the social sciences regarding the healing power of forgiveness. One such researcher is Robert Enright, professor of educational psychology at the University of Wisconsin-Madison, whose work, with the assistance of various associates, is now widely touted. *Christianity Today* devoted a lengthy cover story regarding this type of forgiveness research in its first issue in the year 2000.[1]

Enright acknowledged his deep dependence on and appreciation for the writings on forgiveness by theologian Lewis Smedes.

Enright summarizes the *process* of forgiveness:

- Don't deny feelings of hurt, anger, or shame. Rather, acknowledge these feelings and commit yourself to doing something about them.
- Don't just focus on the person who has harmed you, but identify the specific offensive behavior.
- Make a conscious decision not to seek revenge or nurse a grudge and decide instead to forgive. This conversion of the heart is a critical stage toward forgiveness.

- Formulate a rationale for forgiving. For example, "By forgiving I can experience inner healing and move on with my life."
- Think differently about the offense. Try to see things from the offender's perspective.
- Accept the pain you've experienced without passing it off to others, including the offender.
- Choose to extend goodwill and mercy toward the other; wish for the well-being of that person.
- Think about how it feels to be released from a burden or grudge. Be open to emotional relief. Seek meaning in the suffering you have experienced.
- Realize the paradox of forgiveness: As you let go and forgive the offender, you are experiencing release and healing.[2]

It is obvious that one of the most difficult aspects of forgiving an offender, whether a person or a church, is forgiving people who do not say they are sorry. Smedes addresses this problem succinctly, citing six reasons to forgive people who never say they are sorry:

Forgiving is something good we do for ourselves; we should not have to wait for permission from the person who did something bad to us.

When we forgive someone who does not say he's sorry, we are not issuing him a welcome back to the relationship we had before; if he wants to come back he must come in sorrow.

To *give* forgiveness requires nothing but a desire to be free of our resentment. To *receive* forgiveness requires sorrow for what we did to give someone reason to be resentful.

We cannot *expect* to be forgiven without sorrow for the wrong we did. We should not *demand* sorrow for the wrong someone did to us.

Repentance does not earn the right to forgiveness; it only prepares us to receive the gift.

A wounded person should not put her future happiness in the hands of the person who made her miserable.[3]

When I was pressured to retire early in my last pastorate by the machinations of a small group of antagonists, I wrote each one a lengthy personal letter describing how I felt about what they did to me, my ministry, my marriage, my family, my health, and my future. I tried to be honest without being harsh. I felt they needed to know that they had hurt me deeply. Not one of them wrote in response, called me, or came by for a visit. Not one said he was sorry. Therefore, I had to move on with my life, shattered though it was, and start over somewhere else.

For my own sake, I needed to forgive them even though none said he was sorry. I tried to do that even though it took me a long time. I wrote to each one that I was forgiving him of his mistreatment of me, knowing it would be a process rather than something instantaneous. I had to do it for myself. I did not expect reconciliation, but I did need to be free of my resentment. I did not expect sorrow or repentance from them in order to forgive them. I made a distinct decision not to seek revenge. There were several things I could have done, but I chose not to do any of those vengeful acts. I could not afford to put my future happiness in the hands of those people who made me so miserable by their abuse of me.[4]

Preach the Gospel, Not Your Wounds

If an abusive situation forces you to "shake the dust off your feet" and go elsewhere, then do it. The story is told that Winston Churchill was once asked to speak at a graduation commencement at Oxford University in the late years of his tumultuous life full of both victories and defeats. As he rose to speak, he uttered only one sentence: "Never give up!" His booming voice probably still resonates in the memories of those graduates.

Wounded ministers need to hear the voice of God boom forth those same words: "Never give up!" For as long as you have breath and your heart beats, you have a message of Good News to proclaim. So preach it, but as you do so, don't preach your wounds. That is, don't let any bitterness, resentment, or anger muddy the waters of your message.

Rather, in a renewed ministry become a wounded healer!

And, "Never give up!"

Notes

Chapter 1: *Clergy Killers on the Loose*

1. G. Lloyd Rediger, *Clergy Killers: Guidance for Pastors and Congregations under Attack* (Louisville, Ky.: Westminster/John Knox, 1997).
2. Ibid., 1.
3. Ibid., 8.
4. Ibid., 9.
5. M. Scott Peck, *People of the Lie: The Hope for Healing Human Evil* (New York: Simon & Schuster, 1983).
6. Mike Clingenpeel, "Baptists Need a Cure for Church Rage," *Baptist Standard* (14 October 1998): 5.
7. Ken Coffee, "The Abusive Congregation," *Baptist Standard* (21 June 1995): 12.

Chapter 2: *Pathological Antagonists in the Church*

1. Kenneth C. Haugk, *Antagonists in the Church: How to Identify and Deal with Destructive Conflict* (Minneapolis: Augsburg, 1988), 21–22. The following section is adapted from Haugk, 26–27.
2. Ibid., 26.
3. Ibid., 27.
4. Ibid., 27–30.
5. Marshall Shelley, *Well-Intentioned Dragons: Ministering to Problem People in the Church* (Minneapolis: Bethany, 1985).
6. See church conflict resolution consultant Speed Leas's treatment of this in his *Moving Your Church through Conflict* (Washington, D.C.: The Alban Institute, 1985).
7. Haugk, *Antagonists in the Church*, 38–39.

Chapter 3: *When Evil Invades the Church*

1. Rediger, *Clergy Killers*, 19–20; italics added.
2. Ron Susek, *Firestorm: Preventing and Overcoming Church Conflicts* (Grand Rapids: Baker, 1999).

3. M. Scott Peck, *The Road Less Traveled: A New Psychology of Love, Traditional Values and Spiritual Growth* (New York: Simon & Schuster, 1978).

4. Peck, *People of the Lie*, 129.

5. Ibid., 76.

6. Ibid., 77.

7. Ibid., 77–78. See also C. M. Berry's articles on these subjects in *Baker Encyclopedia of Psychology and Counseling*, 2d ed., eds. David G. Benner and Peter C. Hill (Grand Rapids: Baker, 1999), 780–83.

8. Peck, *People of the Lie*, 79.

9. David L. Goetz, "Forced Out," *Leadership* XVII, no. 1 (winter 1996): 42.

10. David F. Wells, *Losing Our Virtue: Why the Church Must Recover Its Moral Vision* (Grand Rapids: Eerdmans, 1998), 74.

Chapter 4: *The Minister's Greatest Enemy: Passive Lay Leaders*

1. Quoted in Scott B. Rae and Kenman L. Wong, *Beyond Integrity: A Judeo-Christian Approach to Business Ethics* (Grand Rapids: Zondervan, 1996), 117.

2. Shakespeare, *Julius Caesar*, act III, sc. 1, line 77.

3. Samuel Taylor Coleridge, *The Rime of the Ancient Mariner*, part IV, stanza 3; part VI, stanza 10; part VII, stanza 19.

Chapter 5: *The Dangers of Autonomous Church Polity*

1. See Robertson's comments on Rom. 16:1 as well as his insights on 1 Tim. 3:11 in his *Word Pictures in the New Testament* (Nashville: Broadman, 1931), vol. IV, 425, 575.

Chapter 6: *Wrecking a Minister's Life and Career*

1. An excellent general treatment of this problem is Jeff VanVonderen, *When God's People Let You Down: How to Rise above the Hurts That Often Occur within the Church* (Minneapolis: Bethany, 1995).

2. Such referral sources include The Alban Institute, 7315 Wisconsin Avenue, Suite 1250W, Bethesda, MD 20814-3211, or call 1-800-486-1318, X-230; and Ministering to Ministers Foundation, Inc., 2641 Cromwell Road, Richmond, VA 23235, or call 1-804-320-6463, see web site http://www.bengtson.org/mtm, or e-mail MTMFound@aol.com.

Chapter 7: *Collateral Damage to Ministers*

1. Howard Clinebell, *Basic Types of Pastoral Care and Counseling* (Nashville: Abingdon, 1984), 188–90.

2. See Thomas H. Holmes and R. H. Rahe, "The Social Adjustment Ratings Scale," *Journal of Psychosomatic Research* 2 (1967): 213–18. See also T. H. Holmes and M. Masudu, "Life Change and Illness Suscepti-bility," in Barbara Snell Dohrenwend and Bruce P. Dohrenwend, eds., *Stressful Life Events* (New York: Wiley, 1974), 42–72.

3. Daniel A. Girdano and George S. Everly Jr., *Controlling Stress and Tension: A Holistic Approach*, 2d ed. (Englewood Cliffs, N.J.: Prentice-Hall, 1986), 1–7. See Gary R. Collins, *Spotlight on Stress* (Ventura, Calif.: Vision House, 1982), 11–24.

4. Brooks R. Faulkner, comp., *Stress in the Life of the Minister* (Nashville: Convention Press, 1981); Brooks R. Faulkner, *Burnout in Ministry: How to Recognize It, How to Avoid It* (Nashville: Broadman, 1981).

5. For further information, write to: D/ART/Public Inquiries, National Institute of Mental Health, Room 10-85, 5600 Fishers Lane, Rockville, MD 20857. For a professional discussion of depression, see the appropriate listings in *Diagnostic and Statistical Manual of Mental Disorders*, 4th ed. (commonly referred to as DSM-IV) (Washington, D.C.: American Psychiatric Association, 1994).

6. For a classic treatment of this subject see the symposium of Wayne E. Oates, ed., *The Minister's Own Mental Health* (Great Neck, N.Y.: Channel Press, 1961). Although out of print, copies may be found in most seminary and religious university libraries.

7. C. Welton Gaddy, *A Soul under Siege: Surviving Clergy Depression* (Louisville, Ky.: Westminster/John Knox, 1991).

8. Harold S. Kushner, *When Bad Things Happen to Good People* (New York: Schocken Books, 1981).

9. David Elton Trueblood, *Philosophy of Religion* (New York: Harper & Brothers, 1957), 231–56.

Chapter 8: *Collateral Damage to the Church*

1. Even Brooks Faulkner, the noted expert on this problem, gives only general observations of damage in his classic *Forced Termination: Redemptive Options for Ministers and Churches* (Nashville: Broadman, 1986).

2. John C. LaRue Jr., "Forced Exits: High-Risk Churches," *Your Church* (May/June 1996): 72.

Chapter 9: *Ministers Who Invite Attack*

1. The topic of the abusive minister can be found in articles published in various denominational papers. As an example, see Ken Coffee, "The Abusive Minister," *Baptist Standard* (5 July 1995): 18.

2. Karen Horney, *The Neurotic Personality of Our Time* (New York: W. W. Norton, 1937), 14–15.

3. H. A. Selvey, "Neurosis," in *Dictionary of Pastoral Care and Counseling*, ed. Rodney J. Hunter (Nashville: Abingdon Press, 1990), 784–85.

4. Adapted from James Morrison, *DSM-IV Made Easy: The Clinician's Guide to Diagnosis* (New York: Guilford Press, 1995), 485–86. Morrison's source was *Diagnostic and Statistical Manual of Mental Disorders*, 4th ed. (Washington, D.C.: American Psychiatric Association, 1994): 658–61, commonly referred to as DSM-IV.

5. Morrison, *DSM-IV Made Easy*, 483.

6. Ibid., 482.

7. Suellen Fried and Paula Fried, *Bullies and Victims: Helping Your Child Survive the Schoolyard Battlefield* (New York: M. Evans and Company, 1996). Some of these childhood bullies grow up to become bully ministers.

8. The following books appeared during the past decade: Lynn Weiss, *Attention Deficit Disorder in Adults*, 3d ed. (Dallas: Taylor Publishing, 1997); Kate Kelly and Peggy Ramundo, *You Mean I'm Not Lazy, Stupid or Crazy?! A Self-Help Book for Adults with Attention Deficit Disorder* (New York: Scribner, 1993); Edward M. Hallowell and John J. Ratey, *Driven to Distraction: Recognizing and Coping with Attention Deficit Disorder from Childhood through Adulthood* (New York: Simon & Schuster, 1994).

9. Note that some ADD persons have a hyperactive element; these are referred to as ADHD (Attention Deficit Hyperactive Disorder). However, the hyperactive element found among some children tends to change when they become adults from physical hyperactivity to verbal hyperactivity; i.e., rapid, choppy speech patterns.

10. Adapted from Kelly and Ramundo, *You Mean I'm Not Lazy, Stupid or Crazy?!* 10–15.

11. Hallowell and Ratey, *Driven to Distraction*, 237–44.

12. Peter Gorner, "Study Traces Hyperactivity to a Specific Gene," *Amarillo Daily News* (3 April 1995): 6A. This story is a Knight-Ridder News Service release reporting the discovery from the University of Chicago by psychiatrists Edwin Cook, Mark Stein, and colleagues.

13. Especially helpful is Lynn Weiss, *A.D.D. on the Job: Making Your A.D.D. Work for You* (Dallas: Taylor Publishing, 1996).

14. Henry Cloud and John Townsend, *The Mom Factor: Dealing with the Mother You Had, Didn't Have, or Still Contend With* (Grand Rapids: Zondervan, 1996), see especially chapter 6, "The Controlling Mom."

15. For an excellent treatment of this subject, see Howard Clinebell, *Understanding and Counseling Persons with Alcohol, Drug, and Behavioral Addictions*, rev. ed. (Nashville: Abingdon Press, 1998), 424–30.

16. R. J. Salinger, "Depression: Physiological Factors," in *Baker Encyclopedia of Psychology*, David S. Benner, ed. (Grand Rapids: Baker, 1985), 306–7.

17. DSM-IV, 732.

18. W. W. Austin, "Minnesota Multiphasic Personality Inventory (MMPI)" in *Baker Encyclopedia of Psychology*, Benner, ed., 717–18; Douglas N. Jackson et al., *Basic Personality Inventory, Manual*, 2d ed. (Port Huron, Mich.: Sigma Assessment Systems, Inc., 1996); M. P. Maloney, "Evaluation and Diagnosis, Psychological" in *Dictionary of Pastoral Care and Counseling*, Hunter, ed., 366–71.

Chapter 10: *Abuse from Pathological Ministers*

1. The classic work on type A behavior was by Meyer Friedman, *Type A Behavior: Its Diagnosis and Treatment* (New York: Plenum, 1996). A more popular version is Meyer Friedman and Diane Ulmer, *Treating Type A Behavior and Your Heart* (New York: Ballantine Books, 1985). Type A refers to the uptight, driven person, while type B refers to the laid-back, easygoing individual.

2. Morrison, *DSM-IV Made Easy*, 464.

3. Ibid., 478–80.

4. Ibid., 483.

5. Ibid., 485–86.

6. Ibid., 493–94.

7. Wayne E. Oates, *Behind the Masks: Personality Disorders in Religious Behavior* (Philadelphia: Westminster Press, 1987), 12.

Chapter 11: *A Ministers' Advisory Council*

1. For an excellent discussion of administering personnel policies and job descriptions for a church, see Bruce P. Powers, ed., *Church Administration Hand-Book*, rev. ed. (Nashville: Broadman & Holman, 1997), 21–55, 71–97.

Chapter 12: *Steps toward Healing for Abused Clergy*

1. Leo Madow, *Anger: How to Recognize and Cope with It* (New York: Scribners, 1972), 71.

2. This is thoroughly documented by psychologist Blair Justice in *Who Gets Sick: How Belief, Moods, and Thoughts Affect Your Health* (Los Angeles: Jeremy P. Tarcher, 1988); also see the fascinating work of oncologist Bernie S. Siegel, *Love, Medicine, and Miracles* (New York: Harper & Row, 1986), who discovered the destructive role of anger in selected cancer patients.

3. Redford and Virginia Williams, *Anger Kills: Seventeen Strategies for Controlling the Hostility That Can Harm Your Health* (New York: Harper-Collins, 1994), 45–52.

4. For an in-depth study of loneliness in the ministry and its effect on a minister's marriage, see Janelle Warner and John D. Carter, "Loneliness, Marital Adjustment and Burnout in Pastoral and Lay Persons," *Journal of Psychology and Theology* 12 (summer 1984): 125–31.

Another superb treatment of dealing with loneliness is Gary Collins, *Christian Counseling: A Comprehensive Guide*, rev. ed. (Dallas: Word, 1988), 92–103.

5. Dr. Lewis McBurney, a psychiatrist, and his wife, Melissa, of Carbondale, Colorado (near Glenwood Springs) Marble Retreat, 139 Bannock Burn, Carbondale, CO 81623, 970-963-2499; and Dr. Walter Becker and his wife, Fran, both clinical psychologists, of Alto, New Mexico (near Ruidoso)1 Gray Box Lane, Alto, NM 88312, 505-336-7721, are some Christian therapists with whom I am familiar. These retreat experiences can be tremendously helpful.

6. An excellent discussion of ministry peer support groups may be found in chapter 10, "Building Support," by Roy M. Oswald, in *Surviving Ministry: Navigating the Pitfalls, Experiencing the Renewals*, eds. Robert R. Lutz and Bruce T. Taylor (New York: Paulist Press, 1990), 98–107.

7. This list is adapted from Emrika Padus et al., *The Complete Guide to Your Emotions and Your Health: New Dimensions in Mind/Body Healing* (Emmaus, Pa.: Rodale Press, 1986), 154.

8. Lewis B. Smedes, *The Art of Forgiving: When You Need to Forgive and Don't Know How* (New York: Ballantine Books, 1996); see also Lewis B. Smedes, *Forgive and Forget: Healing the Hurts We Don't Deserve* (Carmel, N.Y.: Guideposts, 1984).

9. Hunter, ed., *Dictionary of Pastoral Care and Counseling*, 438.

10. Smedes, *The Art of Forgiving*, 3–12.

11. Ibid., 13–21.

12. Ibid., 18.

13. Ibid., 27.

14. Ibid., 45.

15. Ibid., 65–74.

16. William R. Miller and Kathleen A. Jackson, *Practical Psychology for Pastors*, 2d ed. (Englewood Cliffs: Prentice-Hall, 1995), 296–97.

17. Ibid., 296.

Chapter 13: *Recovering from Shattered Dreams*

1. For a shocking contemporary experience of a minister being stalked by a pathological antagonist couple from his previous church, see Haugk, *Antagonists in the Church*, 27–28.

2. If such courses cannot be found, secure a copy of David D. Burns, *Ten Days to Self-Esteem* (New York: William Morrow, 1993); this work-

book is especially adapted for individual use. For group study of Dr. Burns's cognitive therapy principles, use David D. Burns, *Ten Days to Self-Esteem: The Leader's Manual* (New York: William Morrow, 1993). This program was pilot tested in churches as well as in hospitals, schools, and business settings.

3. For an inspiring account of Robert Schuller's ministry, see James Penner, *Goliath: The Life of Robert Schuller* (Anaheim, Calif.: New Hope Publishing, 1992). Here is an example of one man who started a new church and ministry and has stayed there all of his life.

4. Mark McMinn, *Cognitive Therapy Techniques in Christian Counseling* in *Resources in Christian Counseling*, ed. Gary R. Collins (Dallas: Word, 1991), 25–32.

5. Adapted from David D. Burns, *Feeling Good: The New Mood Therapy* (New York: William Morrow, 1980), 41–50.

6. Adapted from Burns, *Ten Days to Self-Esteem*, 50–51.

7. See the excellent discussion of how to respond to difficult people in Arthur Paul Boers, *Never Call Them Jerks: Healthy Responses to Difficult Behavior* (Washington, D.C.: Alban Institute, 1999).

Chapter 14: *Wounded Healers*

1. Rediger, *Clergy Killers*, 1.

2. Henri J. M. Nouwen, *The Wounded Healer: Ministry in Contemporary Society* (Garden City, N.Y.: Doubleday, 1972), 83–84.

3. Especially helpful is chapter 14, "Group Care and Counseling" in Clinebell, *Basic Types of Pastoral Care and Counseling*, 349–72; also useful are Johnny Jones, comp., *Life Support: Your Church's Lifeline to Hurting People, Leader's Handbook* (Nashville: LifeWay Press, 1993), and Jimmy Long et al., ed., *Small Group Leaders' Handbook* (Downers Grove, Ill.: InterVarsity Press, 1995).

See also the article "Group Dynamics" by Martin Bolt in *Baker Encyclopedia of Psychology and Counseling*, 2d ed., eds. Benner and Hill, 523–25. Also see the article "Group Dynamics, Process, and Research" in *Dictionary of Pastoral Care and Counseling*, ed., Hunter, 481–83. These reference works ought to be in every minister's library.

4. Jeffrey Weiss, "Wounded Heroes," *Dallas Morning News,* 7 March 1998, sec. G1, p. 3.

5. Toby Druin, "Gage Hopes to Redeem 'Wounded Heroes,'" *Baptist Standard* (17 December 1997): 3.

6. Toby Druin, "'Heroes' Tell of Struggles to Regain Worth," *Baptist Standard* (31 March 1999): 12.

Afterword: *Growing through Rejection*

1. Gary Thomas, "The Forgiveness Factor," *Christianity Today* (10 January 2000): 38–45.

2. Ibid., 43.

3. Smedes, *The Art of Forgiving*, 93–94.

4. For further study, see Robert D. Enright and Joanna North, ed., *Exploring Forgiveness* (Madison: University of Wisconsin Press, 1998). This work contains an excellent bibliography on forgiveness literature and research, including material on forgiveness from a Christian, theological perspective. Also, check the following web sites: Campaign for Forgiveness Research: http://www.forgiving.org, and International Forgiveness Institute: http://www.intl-forgive-inst.org.

Recommended Reading

The author has found the following books extremely helpful in dealing with the topic of wounded ministers. Each one offers the reader unusual insights into the various aspects of being wounded in the ministry.

Bagby, Daniel G. *Understanding Anger in the Church*. Nashville: Broadman Press, 1979.

Boers, Arthur Paul. *Never Call Them Jerks: Healthy Responses to Difficult Behavior*. Washington, D.C.: Alban Institute, 1999.

Carter, Jay. *Nasty People: How to Stop Being Hurt by Them without Becoming One of Them*. Chicago: Contemporary Books, 1989.

Chandler, Charles H. *Minister's Support Group: Alternative to Burnout*. Nashville: Convention Press, 1987.

Crowell, Rodney J. *Musical Pulpits: Clergy and Laypersons Face the Issue of Forced Exits*. Grand Rapids: Baker, 1992.

Faulkner, Brooks R. *Burnout in Ministry: How to Recognize It, How to Avoid It*. Nashville: Broadman Press, 1981.

———. *Forced Termination: Redemptive Options for Ministers and Churches*. Nashville: Broadman Press, 1986.

Gaddy, C. Welton. *Soul under Siege: Surviving Clergy Depression*. Louisville, Ky.: Westminster/John Knox, 1991.

Haugk, Kenneth C. *Antagonists in the Church: How to Identify and Deal with Destructive Conflict*. Minneapolis: Augsburg, 1988.

Leas, Speed. *Moving Your Church through Conflict*. Washington, D.C.: Alban Institute, 1985.

London, H. B., and Neil B. Wiseman. *Pastors at Risk: Help for Pastors, Hope for the Church*. Wheaton, Ill.: Victor Books, 1993.

Marshall, Myra, with Dan McGee and Jennifer Bryon Owen. *Beyond Termination: A Spouse's Story of Pain and Healing*. Nashville: Broadman, 1990.

McIntosh, Gary L., and Samuel D. Rima Sr. *Overcoming the Dark Side of Leadership: The Paradox of Personal Dysfunction*. Grand Rapids: Baker, 1997.

McSwain, Larry L., and William C. Treadwell Jr. *Conflict Ministry in the Church*. Nashville: Broadman Press, 1981. Second printing by The Ministerial Association, General Conference of Seventh-day Adventists, Silver Spring, Md., 1997.

Miller, Michael D. *Honoring the Ministry: Honoring the Leaders God Gives Your Church*. Nashville: LifeWay Press, 1998.

Oates, Wayne E. *Behind the Masks: Personality Disorders in Religious Behavior*. Philadelphia: Westminster Press, 1987.

———. *The Care of Troublesome People*. Washington, D.C.: Alban Institute, 1994.

Rediger, G. Lloyd. *Clergy Killers: Guidance for Pastors and Congregations under Attack*. Louisville, Ky.: Westminster/John Knox, 1997.

Shelley, Marshall. *Well-Intentioned Dragons: Ministering to Problem People in the Church*. Minneapolis: Bethany, 1985.

Smedes, Lewis B. *The Art of Forgiving: When You Need to Forgive and Don't Know How*. New York: Ballantine Books, 1996.

Solomon, Muriel. *Working with Difficult People*. Englewood Cliffs, N.J.: Prentice-Hall, 1990.

Susek, Ron. *Firestorm: Preventing and Overcoming Church Conflicts*. Grand Rapids: Baker, 1999.

VanVonderen, Jeff. *When God's People Let You Down: How to Rise above the Hurts That Often Occur within the Church*. Minneapolis: Bethany, 1995.

Warren, Neil Clark. *Make Anger Your Ally: Harnessing One of Your Most Powerful Emotions*. Brentwood, Tenn.: Wolgemuth and Hyatt, 1990.

Guy Greenfield holds his doctorate from Southwestern Baptist Theological Seminary, where he was also a professor of Christian Eithics for over a decade. He also pastored several Southern Baptist churches in Texas and is the author of several books, most recently *The Wounded Parent* and *Re-Igniting Love and Passion.* Since leaving the pastorate he has founded Panhandle Pastoral Counseling Ministry in Amarillo, Texas, where he provides counseling services in cooperation with churches that do not have their own counseling staff available.